FEDERAL RESPONSES TO DOMESTIC VIOLENCE

THE FAMILY VIOLENCE PREVENTION AND SERVICES ACT AND THE VIOLENCE AGAINST WOMEN ACT

SOCIAL ISSUES, JUSTICE AND STATUS

Additional books in this series can be found on Nova's website
under the Series tab.

Additional E-books in this series can be found on Nova's website
under the E-book tab.

CRIMINAL JUSTICE, LAW ENFORCEMENT AND CORRECTIONS

Additional books in this series can be found on Nova's website
under the Series tab.

Additional E-books in this series can be found on Nova's website
under the E-book tab.

SOCIAL ISSUES, JUSTICE AND STATUS

FEDERAL RESPONSES TO DOMESTIC VIOLENCE

THE FAMILY VIOLENCE PREVENTION AND SERVICES ACT AND THE VIOLENCE AGAINST WOMEN ACT

SARA P. ZIMMERMAN
EDITOR

New York

LIBRARY OF CONGRESS CATALOGING-IN-PUBLICATION DATA

ISBN: 978-1-62618-951-5

Published by Nova Science Publishers, Inc. † *New York*

CONTENTS

PREFACE

Family violence broadly refers to acts of physical and sexual violence and emotional abuse perpetrated by individuals against family members. The federal government has responded to various forms of family violence, including violence involving spouses and other intimate partners, children, and the elderly. The focus of this book is on the federal response to domestic violence under the Family Violence Prevention and Services Act (FVPSA). "Domestic violence" is used in this book to describe violence among intimate partners, including those involved in dating relationships. A survey conducted by the Centers for Disease Control (CDC) found that approximately 7 million women and 5.7 million men experienced physical violence, rape, and/or stalking by their intimate partners in 2010. Also that year, 16.6 million women and 20.5 million men experienced emotional abuse by their intimate partners, such as attempting to keep victims from communicating with loved ones. Domestic violence is associated with multiple negative outcomes for victims, including mental and physical health effects.

Chapter 1 – Family violence broadly refers to acts of physical and sexual violence and emotional abuse perpetrated by individuals against family members. The federal government has responded to various forms of family violence, including violence involving spouses and other intimate partners, children, and the elderly. The focus of this report is on the federal response to domestic violence under the Family Violence Prevention and Services Act (FVPSA). "Domestic violence" is used in the report to describe violence among intimate partners, including those involved in dating relationships. A survey conducted by the Centers for Disease Control (CDC) and Prevention found that approximately 7 million women and 5.7 million men (5.9% and 5.0% of all women and men, respectively) experienced physical violence, rape, and/or stalking by their intimate partners in 2010. Also that year, 16.6 million women (13.9%) and 20.5 million men (18.1%) experienced emotional abuse by their intimate partners, such as attempting to keep victims from communicating with loved ones. Domestic violence is associated with multiple negative outcomes for victims, including mental and physical health effects.

Throughout much of the 20th century, domestic violence remained a hidden problem. Survivors of this abuse often endured physical and emotional abuse in silence out of fear of retaliation by their spouses and other intimate partners. In the 1970s, former battered women, civic organizations, and professionals began to open shelters and provide services to abused women and their children. As a result of these efforts and greater national attention to domestic violence, Congress conducted a series of hearings in the early 1980s to understand the scope of this violence and explore possible responses. In 1984, Congress passed FVPSA (Title III of P.L. 98-457). FVPSA has been reauthorized seven times, most recently through FY2015 (P.L. 111-320).

Congress appropriates funding for three sets of activities under FVPSA to address domestic violence. First, a national domestic violence hotline receives calls for assistance related to this violence. The hotline maintains a database of services throughout the United States and territories, and it provides referrals for victims and others affected by family violence. Second, FVPSA supports direct services to victims and their families, including victims in underserved and minority communities and children exposed to domestic violence. Most of this funding is awarded via grants to states, territories, and tribes, which then distribute the funds to local domestic violence service organizations. These organizations provide shelter and a number of services—counseling, referrals, development of a safety plan, advocacy, legal advocacy, and other services. This funding also supports state domestic violence coalitions that provide training for service providers and advocacy for victims, and nine national resource centers that provide training and technical assistance on various family violence issues for a variety of stakeholders. Third, FVPSA funds efforts to prevent domestic violence through a program known as Domestic Violence Prevention Enhancement and Leadership Through Allies (DELTA). DELTA supports coordinated efforts in local communities primarily in 14 states. FVPSA activities are administered by the U.S. Department of Health and Human Services (HHS), and were funded at $138.1 million in FY2012.

Enacted in 1984, FVPSA was the first federal law to address domestic violence. It has continued to have a primary focus on providing shelter and services for survivors, and has increasingly provided support to children exposed to domestic violence and teen dating violence. Since the 1994 enactment of the Violence Against Women Act (VAWA), the federal response to domestic violence has expanded to include investigating and prosecuting crimes and providing additional services to victims and abusers. VAWA activities are administered by multiple federal agencies.

Chapter 2 – In 1994, Congress passed the Violence Against Women Act (VAWA, P.L. 103-322). The act was intended to change attitudes toward domestic violence, foster awareness of domestic violence, improve services and provisions for victims, and revise the manner in which the criminal justice system responds to domestic violence and sex crimes. The legislation created new programs within the Departments of Justice and Health and Human Services that aimed to reduce domestic violence and improve response to and recovery from domestic violence incidents. VAWA primarily addresses certain types of violent crime through grant programs to state, tribal, and local governments; nonprofit organizations; and universities. VAWA programs target the crimes of intimate partner violence, dating violence, sexual assault, and stalking.

In 1995, the Office on Violence Against Women (OVW) was created administratively within the Department of Justice to administer federal grants authorized under VAWA. In 2002, Congress codified the OVW as a separate office within the Department of Justice (DOJ). Since its creation, the OVW has awarded more than $4.7 billion in grants. While the OVW administers the majority of VAWA authorized grants, other federal agencies, including the Centers for Disease Control and Prevention and the Office of Justice Programs, also manage VAWA grants.

Since 1994, VAWA has been modified and reauthorized several times. In 2000, Congress reauthorized the programs under VAWA, enhanced federal domestic violence and stalking penalties, added protections for abused foreign nationals, and created programs for elderly and disabled women. In 2005, Congress again reauthorized VAWA. In addition to reauthorizing the programs under VAWA, the legislation enhanced penalties for repeat stalking offenders; added additional protections for battered and trafficked foreign nationals; and created programs for sexual assault victims and American Indian victims of domestic violence and related crimes; and created programs designed to improve the public health response to domestic violence.

Authorization for appropriations for the programs under VAWA expired in 2011. VAWA programs are currently unauthorized; however, programs have continued to receive appropriations. In the 112th Congress, bills (S. 1925 and H.R. 4970) were passed in each chamber that would have reauthorized most of the programs under VAWA, among other things. H.R. 4970 differed in substantive ways from S. 1925, including with respect to the VAWA-related immigration provisions, the authority it would have given Indian tribes to enforce domestic violence and related crimes against non-Indian individuals, and in the populations it would have included under its definition of underserved population. Neither bill was enacted into law.

In the 113th Congress, two bills (H.R. 11 and S. 47) have been introduced that would reauthorize most of the programs under VAWA, among other things. On February 12, 2013, the Senate passed S. 47 as amended. The Senate amended S. 47 so the bill would amend and authorize appropriations for the Trafficking Victims Protection Act of 2000, enhance measures to combat trafficking in persons, and amend VAWA grant purpose areas to include sex trafficking. Aside from these amendments, S. 47 and H.R. 11 are similar. A description of these bills is provided in this report.

H.R. 11 and S. 47 contain many of the same provisions that were in reauthorization bills from the 112th Congress. These bills would reauthorize most VAWA grant programs and authorize appropriations at a lower level. Like S. 1925, these bills propose new provisions for certain populations such as American Indian tribes. Both bills would grant authority to Indian tribes to enforce domestic violence and related crimes against non-Indian individuals.

H.R. 11 and S. 47 also differ from reauthorization bills from the 112th Congress. The 113th bills include new provisions to address the rape kit backlog by amending the DNA Analysis Backlog Elimination Act of 2000 (P.L. 106-546). As mentioned, S. 47 now includes provisions that would address trafficking in persons. Additionally, some items that *had* been included in reauthorization bills from the 112th Congress are *not* included in H.R. 11 and S. 47, such as the proposal (in S. 1925 only) to temporarily increase the cap on the number of U visas available for abused foreign nationals (from 10,000 to 15,000). These issues and others are discussed in this report.

In: Federal Responses to Domestic Violence   ISBN: 978-1-62618-951-5
Editor: Sara P. Zimmerman   © 2013 Nova Science Publishers, Inc.

Chapter 1

FAMILY VIOLENCE PREVENTION AND SERVICES ACT (FVPSA): BACKGROUND AND FUNDING*

Adrienne L. Fernandes-Alcantara

SUMMARY

Family violence broadly refers to acts of physical and sexual violence and emotional abuse perpetrated by individuals against family members. The federal government has responded to various forms of family violence, including violence involving spouses and other intimate partners, children, and the elderly. The focus of this report is on the federal response to domestic violence under the Family Violence Prevention and Services Act (FVPSA). "Domestic violence" is used in the report to describe violence among intimate partners, including those involved in dating relationships. A survey conducted by the Centers for Disease Control (CDC) and Prevention found that approximately 7 million women and 5.7 million men (5.9% and 5.0% of all women and men, respectively) experienced physical violence, rape, and/or stalking by their intimate partners in 2010. Also that year, 16.6 million women (13.9%) and 20.5 million men (18.1%) experienced emotional abuse by their intimate partners, such as attempting to keep victims from communicating

---

* This is an edited, reformatted and augmented version of the Congressional Research Service Publication, CRS Report for Congress R42838, dated November 27, 2012.

with loved ones. Domestic violence is associated with multiple negative outcomes for victims, including mental and physical health effects.

Throughout much of the 20th century, domestic violence remained a hidden problem. Survivors of this abuse often endured physical and emotional abuse in silence out of fear of retaliation by their spouses and other intimate partners. In the 1970s, former battered women, civic organizations, and professionals began to open shelters and provide services to abused women and their children. As a result of these efforts and greater national attention to domestic violence, Congress conducted a series of hearings in the early 1980s to understand the scope of this violence and explore possible responses. In 1984, Congress passed FVPSA (Title III of P.L. 98-457). FVPSA has been reauthorized seven times, most recently through FY2015 (P.L. 111-320).

Congress appropriates funding for three sets of activities under FVPSA to address domestic violence. First, a national domestic violence hotline receives calls for assistance related to this violence. The hotline maintains a database of services throughout the United States and territories, and it provides referrals for victims and others affected by family violence. Second, FVPSA supports direct services to victims and their families, including victims in underserved and minority communities and children exposed to domestic violence. Most of this funding is awarded via grants to states, territories, and tribes, which then distribute the funds to local domestic violence service organizations. These organizations provide shelter and a number of services—counseling, referrals, development of a safety plan, advocacy, legal advocacy, and other services. This funding also supports state domestic violence coalitions that provide training for service providers and advocacy for victims, and nine national resource centers that provide training and technical assistance on various family violence issues for a variety of stakeholders. Third, FVPSA funds efforts to prevent domestic violence through a program known as Domestic Violence Prevention Enhancement and Leadership Through Allies (DELTA). DELTA supports coordinated efforts in local communities primarily in 14 states. FVPSA activities are administered by the U.S. Department of Health and Human Services (HHS), and were funded at $138.1 million in FY2012.

Enacted in 1984, FVPSA was the first federal law to address domestic violence. It has continued to have a primary focus on providing shelter and services for survivors, and has increasingly provided support to children exposed to domestic violence and teen dating violence. Since the 1994 enactment of the Violence Against Women Act (VAWA), the federal response to domestic violence has expanded to include investigating and prosecuting crimes and providing additional services to victims and abusers. VAWA activities are administered by multiple federal agencies.

INTRODUCTION

This report provides an overview of the federal response to domestic violence—defined broadly to include acts of physical and nonphysical violence against spouses and other intimate partners—through the Family Violence Prevention and Services Act (FVPSA). FVPSA programs are carried out by the Department of Health and Human Services' Administration for Children and Families (ACF) and the Centers for Disease Control and Prevention (CDC). ACF administers most FVPSA programming, including grants to states, territories, and Indian tribes to support local organizations that provide immediate shelter and related assistance for victims of domestic violence and their children. ACF also provides funding for a national domestic violence hotline that responds to over 1.4 million calls each year. Other ACF assistance supports state domestic violence coalitions that provide training for and advocacy on behalf of domestic violence providers within each state; and nine national resource centers that provide training and technical assistance on various family violence issues for a variety of stakeholders. The CDC funds efforts to prevent domestic violence through a program known as Domestic Violence Prevention Enhancement and Leadership Through Allies (DELTA). The House Committee on Education and the Workforce and the Senate Health, Education, Labor and Pension (HELP) Committee have exercised jurisdiction over FVPSA.

The report begins with background on the definitions of domestic violence, family violence, and related terms. This background section also describes the risk factors for domestic violence and estimates of the number of victims. The next section of the report addresses the history leading up to the enactment of FVPSA, and the major components of the act: a national domestic violence hotline, support for domestic violence shelters and non-residential services, and coordination efforts to prevent domestic violence. The report then discusses recent efforts under FVPSA to assist children and youth exposed to domestic violence, including teen dating violence. Finally, it provides an overview of FVPSA's interaction with other federal laws, including the Child Abuse Prevention and Treatment Act (CAPTA) and the Violence Against Women Act (VAWA).[1] FVPSA was the first federal law to address domestic violence, with a focus on providing shelter and services for survivors; however, since the enactment of VAWA in 1994, the federal response to domestic violence has expanded to involve multiple departments and activities that include investigating and prosecuting crimes and providing additional services to victims and abusers. FVPSA also includes provisions that encourage or require program administrators to coordinate FVPSA programs with related programs and research carried out by other federal agencies. The appendixes provide further detail about FVPSA-related definitions, research, and funding.

BACKGROUND

Definitions

For purposes of this report, "domestic violence" is used to describe "family violence" that involves intimate partners and "dating violence," and generally refers to physical and nonphysical violence and emotional abuse perpetrated by individuals among current or former romantic partners.

The FVPSA statute focuses on "family violence," which can involve many types of family relationships and forms of violence. FVPSA defines the term as acts of violence or threatened acts of violence, including forced detention, that result in physical injury against individuals (including elderly individuals) who are legally related by blood or marriage and/or live in the same household.[2] This definition focuses on physical forms of violence and is limited to abusers and victims[3] who live together or are related by blood or marriage; however, researchers and others generally agree that family violence is broad enough to include nonphysical violence and physical violence that occurs outside of an intimate relationship.[4] Such a definition can encompass a range of scenarios—rape and other forms of sexual violence committed by a current or former spouse or intimate partner who may or may not live in the same household; stalking by a current or former spouse or partner; abuse and neglect of elderly family members and children; and psychologically tormenting and controlling a spouse, intimate partner, or other member of the household.

While family violence can encompass child abuse and elder abuse, FVPSA programs focus on individuals abused by their spouses and other intimate partners. Further, FVPSA references the terms "domestic violence" and "dating violence" as they are defined under VAWA, and discusses these terms alongside family violence. The VAWA definition of "domestic violence" encompasses forms of intimate partner violence—involving current and former spouses or individuals who are similarly situated to a spouse, cohabiting individuals, and parents of children—that are outlawed under state or local laws. VAWA defines "dating violence" as violence committed by a person who has been in a social relationship of a romantic or intimate nature with the victim; and where the existence of such a relationship is determined based on consideration of the length of the relationship, the type of relationship, and the frequency of interaction between the individuals involved. (**Table A-1** in **Appendix A** provides a summary of these and related terms.)

The federal government responds to child abuse and elder abuse through a variety of separate programs. Congress authorizes and funds a range of activities to prevent and respond to child abuse and neglect under Titles IV-B and IV-E of the Social Security Act and CAPTA.[5] Separately, the Older Americans Act (OAA), the major federal vehicle for the delivery of social and nutrition services for older persons, has authorized projects to address elder abuse. In addition, the OAA authorizes and Congress funds the National Center on Elder Abuse to provide information to the public and professionals regarding elder abuse prevention activities, and provides training and technical assistance to state elder abuse agencies and to community-based organizations.[6] The Social Services Block Grant, as amended, also includes elder justice provisions, including several grant programs and other activities to promote the safety and well-being of older Americans.[7]

Risk Factors for Domestic Violence

The evidence base on domestic violence does not point strongly to any one reason that it is perpetrated, in part because of the difficulty in measuring social conditions (e.g., status of women, gender norms, and socioeconomic status) that can influence this violence. Still, the research literature has identified two underlying influences: the unequal position of women and the normalization of violence, both in society and some relationships.[8] Certain risk variables are often associated—but not necessarily the causes—of domestic violence. Such factors include a pattern of problem drinking, poverty and economic conditions, and early parenthood.[9] For example, substance abuse often precedes incidents of domestic violence. A study that examined the connection between alcohol and drug use and domestic violence, including homicide or attempted homicide, found that substance abuse was more prevalent among male perpetrators of violence than non-perpetrators; however, the study did not determine how substance use influenced the violence, if at all.[10]

Profiles of Survivors

Estimating the number of individuals involved in domestic violence is complicated by the varying definitions of the term and methodologies for collecting data. For example, some research counts a boyfriend or girlfriend as a family relationship while others do not; still other surveys are limited to specific types of violence and whether violence is reported to police. Certain studies focus more broadly on various types of violence or more narrowly on violence committed among intimate partners. In addition, domestic violence is believed to be underreported. Survivors may be reluctant to disclose their victimization because of shame, embarrassment, fear or belief that they may not receive support from law enforcement.[11]

Overall, two studies—the National Intimate Partner and Sexual Violence Survey (NISVS) and the National Crime Victimization Survey (NCVS) show that violence involving intimate partners is not uncommon, and that both women and men are victimized sexually, physically, and psychologically. Women tend to first be victimized at a younger age than men. Further, minority women and men tend to be victimized at higher rates than whites.

National Intimate Partner and Sexual Violence Survey

The National Intimate Partner and Sexual Violence Survey provides information on the prevalence of domestic violence among individuals during their lifetime and in the past 12 months prior to the survey. The study was fielded for the first time in 2010, and was conducted by the Centers for Disease Control and Prevention.[12] The survey examines multiple aspects of intimate partner violence—including rape, physical violence, stalking, sexual violence other than rape, psychological aggression, and other forms of violence that may or may not be reported as a crime. Selected findings of the report are summarized in **Table B-1** in **Appendix B**. Generally speaking, victims tend to be women; however, a significant share of men are victimized. When asked about their experiences in the 12 months prior to the survey, 5.9% of women and 5.0% of men reported that they had experienced rape, physical violence, and/or stalking by their intimate partner. Just over 2.0% of women (2.3%) and men (2.5%) experienced sexual violence other than rape in the previous year. More men (18.1%) than women (13.9%) experienced any psychological aggression over that one-year period. More than one-third (35.6%) of women and more than one- quarter (28.5%) of men in the United States reported that they experienced rape, physical violence, and/or stalking by an intimate partner in their lifetime.[13]

The NISVS also found that domestic violence tends to occur first among women at a younger age than for men. About seven out of ten women were under the age of 25 (22.4% were ages 11 to 17 and 47.1% were ages 18 to 24). By contrast, men tended to be young adults or adults when first victimized (38.6% were ages 18 to 24 and 30.6% were ages 25 to 34). Women and men of color, particularly American Indians and Alaska Natives, are more likely to experience intimate partner violence. Among women, more than half (53.8%) of women who identify as multi-racial and nearly half (46.0%) who identify as American Indian or Alaska Native reported being victimized by their intimate partners. Similarly, males who identified as American Indian or Alaska Native (45.3%) or multi-racial (39.3%) were more likely than men of other racial and ethnic groups to report being victims of rape, physical violence, and/or stalking by an intimate partner.

National Crime Victimization Survey

The National Crime Victimization Survey is an ongoing survey coordinated by the U.S. Department of Justice's Bureau of Justice Statistics within the Office of Justice Programs. NCVS surveys a nationally representative sample of households. It is the primary source of information on the characteristics of criminal nonfatal victimization and on the number and types of crimes that may or may not be reported to law enforcement authorities. NCVS surveyed respondents about whether they have been victims of a violent crime, including rape/sexual assault, robbery, aggravated assault, and simple assault; and for victims, the relationship to the perpetrator.[14] The survey reports the share of crimes that are committed by an intimate partner (current or former spouses, boyfriends, or girlfriends), other family members, friends/acquaintances, or strangers.

The 2010 survey estimated that 407,700 women and 101,530 men—or 509,230 total—were the victims of intimate partner violence. Violence among intimate partners represented 13.4% of all types of violent crimes. Approximately one out of five (21.9%) women and 5.0% of males reported that they were victims of a crime committed by an intimate partner.[15]

An earlier NCVS study (that was supplemented with homicide data) focused on victims murdered by an intimate partner and on the prevalence of domestic violence by characteristics such as income, marital status, and the presence of children in the home. [16] The study examined changes over time, either 1976 or 1993 to 1998. The study found that the number of female victims of domestic violence declined from 1993 to 1998, from 1.1 million to 900,000 violent offenses. In addition, the number of murders by an intimate partner declined over the period from 1,600 murders in 1976 to 1,317 murders in 1998. Further, NCVS data showed that rates of domestic violence were inversely related to income over the 1993-1998 period, with rates seven times higher among women living in households with the lowest annual income (20.3 per 1,000 females) compared to those with the highest annual income (3.3 per 1,000). Marital status was also found to be associated with domestic violence. The rate of domestic violence was highest among those who were divorced or separated (31.9 per 1,000 females and 6.2 per 1,000 males) compared to those who were never married (11.3 and 1.6) or married (2.6 and 0.5). An equal share of victims (43%) had children under age 12 in the household or did not have children under age 12 in the household; the presence of children was unknown for the remaining victims. (See below for research on children exposed to domestic violence.)

Effects of Domestic Violence

Domestic violence is associated with multiple negative outcomes for victims, including mental and emotional distress and health effects. The 2010 NISVS study found that nearly 3 in 10 (28.8%) women and 1 in 10 (9.9%) men have experienced rape, physical violence, and/or stalking by an intimate partner *and* reported at least one impact as a result of this violence. Both women and men most frequently reported that they felt fearful (25.7% of women and 5.2% of men); exhibited post-traumatic stress symptoms (22.3% and 4.7%); and were concerned for their safety (22.2% and 4.5%). A separate study of domestic violence among welfare recipients in two California counties found that their ability to find work was impaired by their victimization.[17] At the end of one year of participating in welfare-to-work activities, about 1 out of 10 (12%) welfare recipients who experienced serious domestic violence were working at least 26 hours a week, compared to more than a quarter (28%) who did not experience this type of victimization.

DOMESTIC VIOLENCE: DEVELOPMENT OF THE ISSUE

Early marriage laws in the United States permitted men to hit their wives, and throughout much of the 20th century family violence remained a hidden problem.[18] Victims, mostly women, often endured physical and emotional abuse in silence. These victims were hesitant to seek help because of fear of retaliation by their spouses/partners and concerns about leaving their homes, children, and neighborhoods behind. Women were worried that they would be perceived as deviant or mentally unstable or would be unable to get by financially.[19] In addition, victims were often blamed for their abuse, based on stereotypical notions of women (e.g., demanding, aggressive, and "frigid," among other characteristics).

In the 1960s, shelters and services for victims of domestic violence became available on a limited basis; however, these services were not always targeted specifically to victims per se. Social service and religious organizations provided temporary housing for displaced persons generally, which could include homeless and abused women. In addition, a small number of organizations provided services to abused women who were married to alcoholic men. Beginning in the 1970s, the "battered women's movement" began to emerge; it sought to heighten awareness of women who were abused by spouses and partners. The movement developed from influences both abroad and within the United States. In England, the first battered women's shelter, Chiswick Women's Aid, galvanized support for similar types of services. In addition, the feminist movement in the United States increasingly brought greater national attention to the issue.[20]

As part of the battered women's movement, former battered women, civic organizations, and professionals opened shelters and began to provide services to victims, primarily abused women and their children.[21] Shelters were most often located in old homes, at Young Women's Christian Association (YWCA) centers, or housed in institutional settings, such as motels or abandoned orphanages. In addition to providing shelter, groups in the battered women's movement organized coalitions to combine resources for public education on the issue, support groups for the victims, and services that were lacking. For example, the YWCA and Women in Crisis Can Act formed a hotline for abused women in Chicago. These and other groups convened the Chicago Abused Women's Coalition to address concerns about services for battered women. The coalition spoke to hundreds of community groups and professional agencies about battered women's stories, explained the significance of violence, detailed how violence becomes sanctioned, dispelled common myths, and challenged community members to provide funding and other support to assist abused women. The coalition mobilized around passage of a state law to protect women and require police training on family violence, among other accomplishments.

Testimony from Victim of Domestic Violence at a 1984 Hearing by the Select Committee on Children, Youth, and Families

"I met Andy just before I left for New York. He visited me ... often, bringing special treats.... But Andy had a violent streak. During Christmas vacation of my senior year, Andy knocked me out in the front seat of his car and raped me. After graduation from Good Shepherd, I tried to attend G.W. University, but Andy wouldn't leave me alone. He constantly harassed me. I left the university to work in a law office downtown ... [and we] were married June 9, 1962. In March 1963 our daughter was born, 19 months later my son was born.... Andy's violence got progressively worse. He would tie me up and beat me several times a week. But when he started doing this in front of the children, I was determined to get away from him. I was 5 months pregnant when he threatened to kill me and the baby with a knife. I tried to escape and he threw me down the stairs. I called a lawyer who advised me to leave under constructive desertion. I left with my children to Colorado but Andy followed in less than two days and brought us home again. At my insistence, Andy finally agreed to see a psychiatrist. The psychiatrist advised me to leave Andy after Andy attacked him.... On the advice of my psychiatrist and my gynecologist, I admitted myself to Springfield State Hospital ... in order to get both the necessary medical treatment for delivery of the baby and the psychological evaluation that would eventually be necessary to get custody of my children.... A few weeks after leaving the hospital I found a room and a job in Bethesda and began the 3-year battle for custody and divorce.... Andy [had] disappeared with my children."

Source: U.S. House of Representatives, Select Committee on Children, Youth, and Families, "Violence and Abuse in American Families," hearing, 98th Congress, 2nd Session.

Based on a survey in the late 1970s, 111 shelters were believed to have been in every state and across urban, suburban, and rural communities. These shelters generally reported that they provided a safe and secure environment for abused women and their children, emotional support and counseling for abused women, and information on legal rights and assistance with housing, among other supports. Approximately 90 of these shelters fielded over 110,000 calls for assistance in a given year.[22] Around this same time, the public became increasingly aware of domestic violence. In 1983, *Time* magazine published an article, "Wife Beating: The Silent Crime," as part of a series of articles on violence in the United States. The article stated: "There is nothing new about wife beating ... What is new is that in the U.S. wife beating is no longer widely accepted as an inevitable and private matter. The change in attitude, while far from complete, has come about in the past 10 to 15 years as part of the profound transformation of ideas about the roles and rights of women in society."[23] In 1984, then-U.S. Attorney General Benjamin Civiletti established the Department of Justice Task Force on Family Violence, which issued a report examining the scope and impact of domestic violence in America. The report also provided recommendations to improve the nation's law enforcement, criminal justice, and community response to offenses that were previously considered "family matters."[24]

Congressional Response

As a result of efforts by advocates and the Justice Department, Congress began to take an interest in domestic violence issues. The House Select Committee on Children, Youth, and Families conducted a series of hearings in 1983 and 1984 on child abuse and family violence throughout the country, to understand the scope of family violence better and explore possible federal responses to the problem. The committee heard from victims, domestic violence service providers, researchers, law enforcement officials, and other stakeholders about the possible number of victims and the need for additional victim services. In 1984, Congress enacted the Family Violence Prevention and Services Act (FVPSA) as Title III of the Child Abuse Amendments of 1984 (CAPTA, P.L. 98-457).Title I of that law amended the Child Abuse Prevention and Treatment Act (CAPTA), and most of the seven subsequent reauthorizations of FVPSA have occurred as part of legislation that reauthorized CAPTA.[25] This includes the most recent reauthorization (P.L. 111-320), which extends funding authority for FVPSA through FY2015. As discussed later in this report, Congress subsequently broadened the federal response to domestic violence via the Violence Against Women Act, enacted in 1994.

FVPSA OVERVIEW

As originally enacted, FVPSA included both a social service and law enforcement response to preventing and responding to domestic violence. Grants were authorized for states, territories, and Indian tribes to establish and expand programs to prevent domestic violence and provide shelter for victims. In addition, Congress authorized grants to provide training and technical assistance to law enforcement personnel, and this funding was ultimately used to train law enforcement personnel throughout the country.[26] Over time, FVPSA was expanded to include support of other activities—including state domestic violence coalitions and grants that focus on prevention activities; however, authorization of funding for FVPSA law enforcement training grants was discontinued in 1992, just before the 1994 Violence Against Women Act was enacted and included funding authority for this purpose.[27]

As outlined in **Figure 1**, FVPSA currently authorizes three major activities—domestic violence shelters and support, the national domestic violence hotline, and domestic violence prevention activities under a program known as DELTA. The Family and Youth Services Bureau in HHS's Administration for Children and Families administers funding for the domestic violence shelters and support and the hotline. HHS's Centers for Disease Control and Prevention administers the DELTA Program. Funding authorization extends through FY2015.

FUNDING

Table 1 includes funding from FY1993 to FY2013 for the three major FVPSA activities. Overall, appropriations have ranged from about $25.0 million (in FY1993) to $139.0 million (estimate for FY2013). Appropriations for shelter, victim services, and program support increased fourfold from FY1993 to FY2000, peaking at just over $130.0 million in FY2010 and declining to about $129.5 million in FY2011 and FY2012. The estimated FY2013 appropriation is $129.5 million. Appropriations for the hotline have grown from an initial amount of $1.0 million in FY1995 to $3.2 million annually since FY1999. DELTA appropriations have decreased from nearly $6 million in FY1999, the year it was first funded, to $5.4 million in recent years.

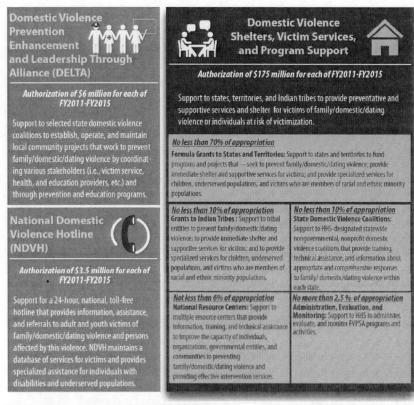

Source: Congressional Research Service (CRS).

Figure 1. Summary of Activities Authorized and Funded Under the Family Violence Prevention and Services Act (FVPSA).

Table 1. Funding for FVPSA Activities, FY1993-FY2013

	Shelter, Services, and Support	National Domestic Violence Hotline	DELTA	Total
FY1993	$24,678,619	N/A	N/A	$24,678,619
FY1994	$32,645,000	N/A	N/A	$32,645,000
FY1995	$32,645,000	$1,000,000	N/A	$33,645,000
FY1996	$47,642,500	$400,000	N/A	$48,042,500
FY1997	$72,800,000	$400,000	N/A	$73,200,000
FY1998	$86,642,206	$1,200,000	N/A	87,842,206
FY1999	$88,778,000	$1,200,000	$5,998,000	$95,976,000

Table 1. (Continued)

	Shelter, Services, and Support	National Domestic Violence Hotline	DELTA	Total
FY2000	$101,118,000	$1,957,000	$5,866,000	$108,941,000
FY2001	$116,899,000	$2,157,000	$5,866,000	$124,922,000
FY2002	$124,459,000	$2,157,000	$5,866,000	$132,482,000
FY2003	$124,459,000	$2,157,000	$5,828,000	$132,444,000
FY2004	$125,648,000	$2,982,000	$5,303,000	$133,933,000
FY2005	$125,630,000	$3,224,000	$5,258,000	$134,112,000
FY2006	$124,643,000	$2,970,000	$5,181,000	$132,794,000
FY2007	$124,731,000	$2,970,000	$5,110,000	$132,811,000
FY2008	$122,552,000	$2,918,000	$5,021,000	$130,491,000
FY2009	$127,776,000	$3,209,000	$5,511,000	$136,496,000
FY2010	$130,052,000[a]	$3,209,000	$5,525,000	$138,786,000
FY2011	$129,792,000	$3,202,000	$5,423,000	$138,417,000
FY2012	$129,547,000	$3,197,000	$5,411,000	$138,155,000
FY2013[b]	$129,547,000	$3,197,000	$5,413,000	$138,157,000

Source: U.S. U.S. Department of Health and Human Services, Administration for Children and Families, *FY1998- FY2013 Justification of Estimates for Appropriations Committees*; and Congressional Research Service correspondence with U.S. Department of Health and Human Services, Administration for Children and Families, Administration on Children, Youth and Families, Family and Youth Services Bureau and Centers for Disease Control and Prevention, September and November 2012; and U.S. Department of Health and Human Services, Administration for Children and Families, *Operating Plan for FY 2013* and Centers for Disease Control, *Operating Plan for FY2013*.

Notes: Funding is allocated for shelter, support services, and program support and the Domestic Violence Hotline via HHS/Administration for Children and Families; and for DELTA via HHS/Centers for Disease Control and Prevention. N/A means not applicable.

a. Funding for FY2010 was just over $130 million ($130,052,000). When FY2010 dollars were appropriated in December 2009, FVPSA required that "a portion of the excess" (of funds for shelter, support services, and program support) above $130 million was to be reserved for projects to address the needs of children who witness domestic violence. FVPSA was reauthorized in December 2010, and this provision was changed to require that when the appropriation exceeds $130 million, HHS must first reserve 25% of the excess funding for specialized services for abused parents and children exposed to domestic violence. This rule was triggered in FY2010 and the excess funding went to a grant program, Expanding Services for Children and Youth Exposed to Domestic Violence. For further information, see the section of this report on children exposed to domestic violence.

b.Funding for FY2013 is provided under the Continuing Appropriations Resolution, 2013 () through March 27, 2013. This extension generally provides an increase of 0.612% over the FY2012 level for most discretionary programs. The law was not accompanied by a conference report or explanatory statement that indicated exact appropriation amount by program. As required under P.L. 112-175, HHS submitted the department's operating plan to the House and Senate Appropriations Committees for funding FY2013 programs through March 27, 2013. Guidance from the Office of Management and Budget (OMB) requires fund to be obligated at the lower of the—(1) percentage of the year covered by the CR (i.e., October 1, 2012 to March 27, 2013 is 48% of the fiscal year) or (2) "historical seasonal rate of obligation" for the period of the year covered by the CR. See U.S. Office of Management and Budget, "Apportionment of the Continuing Resolution(s) for FY2013," OMB Bulletin No. 12-02, September 28, 2012. HHS applied these criteria to their calculations, and the annualized rates are presented in this table.

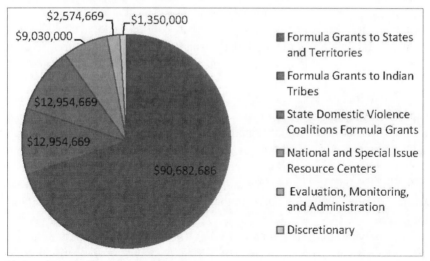

Source: Congressional Research Service.

Figure 2. FY2012 Funding for Shelter, Support Services, and Program Support.

Funding for shelter, support services, and program support encompasses multiple activities: formula grants to states and territories; grants to tribes; state domestic violence coalitions; nine national and special issue resource centers; evaluation, monitoring and administration; and discretionary activities. **Figure 2** displays FY2012 funding for these activities, most of which are described further below.

FORMULA GRANTS TO STATES, TERRITORIES, AND TRIBES

No less than 70% of FVPSA appropriations for shelter and support must be awarded to states and territories through a formula grant. The formula grant supports the establishment, maintenance, and expansion of programs and projects to prevent incidents of domestic violence and to provide shelter and supportive services to victims of domestic violence. Each of the territories— Guam, American Samoa, U.S. Virgin Islands, and the Commonwealth of the Northern Mariana Islands— receives no less than one-eighth of 1% of the appropriation, or, in combination, about one-half of 1% of the total amount appropriated. Of the remaining funds, states (including the District of Columbia and Puerto Rico) receive a base allotment of $600,000 and additional funding based on their relative share of the U.S. population.[28] **Table C-1** in **Appendix C** provides funding in FY2011 and FY2012 for states and territories.

In addition, no less than 10% of FVPSA appropriations for shelter and support are awarded to Indian tribes. Indian tribes have the option to authorize a tribal organization or a nonprofit private organization to submit an application for and to administer FVPSA funds. Nearly all of the same requirements that pertain to states and territories also pertain to tribes. Tribes generally provide the same services, except that they also tend to provide services to both victims and perpetrators.[29] FY2012 funding was $13.0 million for tribes.

In applying for grant funding, states (including territories and Indian tribes) must make certain assurances pertaining to use and distribution of funds and to victims.

Selected Grant Conditions Pertaining to Use and Distribution of Funds[30]

States may use up to 5% of the grant funding for state administrative costs. The remainder of the funds are used to make subgrants to eligible entities for programs and projects that meet the goals of the grant program. No less than 70% of sub-grant funding is to be used to provide shelter, shelter expenses, and programming and services to adult and youth victims of domestic violence and their dependents. Shelter includes the physical space in which victims reside as well as the expenses of running shelter facilities.[31] Related supportive services are listed below. In addition, a minimum of 25% of subgrants must be used for these services.[32]

- Assisting in the development of safety plans, and supporting efforts of victims to make decisions about their ongoing safety and well-being;
- Providing individual and group counseling, peer support groups, and referrals to community-based services to assist victims and their dependents in recovering from the effects of domestic violence;
- Providing services, training, technical assistance, and outreach to increase awareness of domestic violence and increase the accessibility of these services;
- Providing culturally and linguistically appropriate services;
- Providing services for children exposed to domestic violence, including age- appropriate counseling, supportive services, and services for the non-abusing parent that support that parent's role as caregiver (which may include services that work with the non-abusing parent and child together);
- Providing advocacy, case management services, and information and referral services concerning issues related to domestic violence intervention and prevention, including providing assistance in accessing federal and state financial assistance programs; legal advocacy; medical advocacy, including provision of referrals for appropriate health care services (but not reimbursement for any health care services); assistance in locating and securing safe and affordable permanent housing and homelessness prevention services; and transportation, child care, respite care, job training and employment services, financial literacy services and education, financial planning, and related economic empowerment services; parenting and other educational services for victims and their dependents; and
- Providing prevention services, including outreach to underserved populations.[33]

What Are "Eligible Entities" That Can Receive Funding from States/Territories?

A local public agency, or nonprofit private organization—including faith-based and charitable organizations, community-based organizations, tribal organizations, and voluntary associations—that assists victims of domestic violence and their dependents and has a documented history of effective work on this type of violence; *or* a partnership of two or more agencies or organizations that includes an agency or organization described above and an agency or organization that has a demonstrated history of serving populations in their communities, including providing culturally appropriate services.

States must "give special emphasis" to supporting community-based projects of "demonstrated effectiveness" that are carried out by nonprofit organizations that operate shelters for victims of domestic violence and their dependents; or that provide counseling, advocacy, and self-help services to victims. States have discretion in how they allocate their funding, so long as they provide assurances that grant funding will be distributed equitably within the state and between urban and rural areas of the state.

States must also provide assurances that they will consult with and facilitate the participation of state domestic violence coalitions in planning and monitoring the distribution of grants and administering the grants (the role of state domestic violence coalitions is discussed further below). [34] States must describe how they will involve community-based organizations, whose primary purpose is to provide culturally appropriate services to underserved populations, including how such organizations can assist states in meeting the needs of these populations. States must further provide assurances that they have laws or procedures in place to bar an abuser from a shared household or a household of the abused persons, which may include eviction laws or procedures, where appropriate. Such laws or procedures are generally enforced by civil protection orders.

Subgrantees must provide a non-federal match—of not less than $1 for every $5 of federal funding—directly from the state or through donations from public or private entities. [35] The matching funds can be in cash or in kind. Further, federal funds made available to a state must supplement, and not supplant, other federal, state, and local public funds expended on services for victims of domestic violence.

States have two years to spend funds. For example, funds allotted for FY2013 may be spent in FY2013 or FY2014. The HHS Secretary is authorized to reallocate the funds of a state, by the end of the sixth month of a fiscal year that funds are appropriated, if the state fails to meet the requirements of the grant. The Secretary must notify the state if its application for funds has not met these requirements. State domestic violence coalitions are permitted to help determine whether states are in compliance with these provisions. States are allowed six months to correct any deficiencies in their application.

Selected Grant Conditions Pertaining to Victims[36]

Other requirements of the grant program for states address the individual characteristics and privacy of participants and shelters. Both states and subgrantees funded under FVPSA may not deny individuals from participating in support programs on the basis of disability, sex, race, color, national origin, or religion. In addition, states and programs may not impose income eligibility requirements on individuals participating in these programs. Further, states and programs must protect the confidentiality and privacy of victims and their families to help ensure their safety. These entities are prohibited from disclosing any personally identifying information collected about services requested, and from revealing personally identifying information without the consent of the individual, as specified in the law. If the identity of the individual is compelled by statutory or court mandate, states and programs must make reasonable attempts to notify victims, and they must take steps to protect the privacy and safety of the individual. States and programs may share information that has been aggregated and does not identify individuals, and information that has been generated by law enforcement and/or prosecutors and courts pertaining to protective orders or law enforcement and prosecutorial purposes. In addition, the location of confidential shelters may not be made public, except with written authorization of the person(s) operating the shelter. Subgrantees may not provide direct payment to any victim of domestic violence or the dependent(s) of the victim. Further, victims must be provided shelter and services on a voluntary basis. In other words, providers cannot compel or force individuals to come to a shelter, participate in counseling, etc.

STATE DOMESTIC VIOLENCE COALITIONS[37]

Since 1992, FVPSA has authorized funding for state domestic violence coalitions (SDVCs), defined under the act as a statewide nongovernmental, nonprofit private domestic violence organization that (1) has a membership that includes a majority of the primary-purpose domestic violence service providers in the state;[38] (2) has board membership that is representative of domestic violence service providers, and which may include representatives of the communities in which the services are being provided; (3) has as its purpose to provide education, support, and technical assistance to such service providers so they can maintain shelter and supportive services for victims of domestic violence and their dependents; and (4) serves as an information clearinghouse and resource center on domestic violence for the state and supports the development of policies, protocols, and procedures to enhance domestic violence intervention and prevention in the state.

Funding for SDVCs is available for each of the 50 states, the District of Columbia, Puerto Rico, and the four territories (American Samoa, Guam, Commonwealth of the Northern Mariana Islands, and the U.S. Virgin Islands). Each jurisdiction has one SDVC, and these coalitions are designated by HHS. Funding is divided evenly between these 56 jurisdictions. SDVCs must use FVPSA funding for specific activities, as outlined below:

- working with local domestic violence service programs and providers of direct services to encourage appropriate and comprehensive responses to domestic violence against adults or youth within the state, including providing training and technical assistance and conducting needs assessments;
- participating in planning and monitoring the distribution of subgrants and subgrant funds within the state under the grant program for states and territories;
- working in collaboration with service providers and community-based organizations to address the needs of domestic violence victims and their dependents who are members of racial and ethnic minority populations and underserved populations;
- collaborating with and providing information to entities in such fields as housing, health care, mental health, social welfare, or business to support the development and implementation of effective policies, protocols, and programs that address the safety and support needs of adult and youth victims of domestic violence;

- encouraging appropriate responses to cases of domestic violence against adult and youth victims, including by working with judicial and law enforcement agencies;
- working with family law judges, criminal court judges, child protective service agencies, and children's advocates to develop appropriate responses to child custody and visitation issues in cases of child exposure to domestic violence, and in cases where this violence is concurrent with child abuse;
- providing information to the public about prevention of family/domestic/dating violence, including information targeted to underserved populations; and
- collaborating with Indian tribes and tribal organizations (and corresponding Native Hawaiian groups or communities) to address the needs of Indian (including Alaska Native) and Native Hawaiian victims of domestic dating violence, as applicable in the state. [39]

NATIONAL AND SPECIAL ISSUE RESOURCE CENTERS

As originally enacted, FVPSA authorized a national information and research clearinghouse on the prevention of domestic violence. As part of the act's reauthorization in 1992, the language about the clearinghouse was struck and replaced with authorization for resource centers on domestic violence, including resource centers to address key areas of domestic violence. Reauthorization of FVPSA in 2010 included authorization for a national resource center on American Indian women and three culturally specific resources, which had previously been funded through discretionary funds.[40] The 2010 law also authorized resource centers to address disparities of domestic violence in states with high proportions of Indian or Native Hawaiian populations, and training and technical assistance that address emerging issues related to domestic violence.

Pursuant to FVPSA, HHS established the two national resource centers—the National Resource Center on Domestic Violence and the National Indian Resource Center Addressing Domestic Violence and Safety for Indian Women (known as the National Indigenous Women's Resource Center)—and eight special issue resource centers, three of which focus on racial and ethnic minority victims of domestic violence. The purpose of these resource centers is to provide information, training, and technical assistance on domestic violence. This assistance is provided to multiple stakeholders—individuals, organizations, governmental entities, and communities— so that they can improve their capacity for preventing and responding to domestic violence. **Table C-2** summarizes the activities and FY2012 funding for these nine resource centers. The nine centers comprise the Domestic Violence Resource Network (DVRN), which works collaboratively in responding to domestic violence. The DVRN is a project of the National Resource Center on Domestic Violence.

NATIONAL DOMESTIC VIOLENCE HOTLINE[41]

As amended by the Violence Against Women Act (VAWA) in 1994, FVPSA directs the HHS Secretary to award a grant to one or more private entities to operate a 24-hour, national, toll-free hotline on domestic violence. Since 1996, HHS has competitively awarded a cooperative agreement to one organization, the National Council on Family Violence in Texas, to operate the National Domestic Violence Hotline (NDVH).[42] The agreement was most recently awarded in FY2010 for a five-year period ending in FY2014.

FVPSA requires that the hotline provide information and assistance to adult and youth victims of domestic violence, family and household members of victims of such violence, and "persons affected by victimization." As required under FVPSA, the National Council on Family Violence carries out multiple activities:

- It employs, trains, and supervises personnel (paid staff and volunteers) to answer incoming calls; provides counseling and referral services; and directly connects callers to service providers. In FY2011, NVDH received 275,339 calls and answered 207,307 (75.3%) of these calls.[43] The average wait time for a call was 49 seconds. According to HHS, the number of calls to the hotline is increasing as the result of media outreach, public awareness campaigns, and the impact of the recession.[44]
- The National Council on Family Violence maintains a database of domestic violence services for victims throughout the United States, including information on the availability of shelter and services. This database includes information on services for victims of domestic violence, including the availability of shelters to which callers may be referred or directly linked to throughout the United States.

- The National Council on Family Violence provides assistance and referrals for family and household members who are victims and persons affected by victimization. This includes information on domestic violence, children exposed to domestic violence, sexual assault, intervention programs for batterers, and related issues.
- The National Council on Family Violence provides assistance to meet the needs of special populations, including underserved populations (not defined in FVPSA), individuals with disabilities, and youth victims of domestic and dating violence. The hotline provides access to personnel for callers with limited English proficiency and persons who are deaf and hard of hearing. Since 2007, the National Council on Family Violence has operated a separate hotline for youth victims of domestic violence, the National Teen Dating Abuse Helpline.

PREVENTION ACTIVITIES (DELTA)[45]

Since 1994, FVPSA has authorized the HHS Secretary to award cooperative agreements to state domestic violence coalitions that coordinate local community projects to prevent domestic violence, including such violence involving youth. Congress first awarded funding for prevention activities in FY1996 under a pilot program carried out by the CDC. The pilot program was formalized in 2002 under a program now known as the Domestic Violence Prevention Enhancement and Leadership Through Alliances (DELTA) program. The focus of DELTA is preventing domestic violence before it occurs, rather than responding once it happens or working to prevent its recurrence.[46] The program has had three iterations—DELTA, which was funded through FY2012 and involved 14 states; DELTA Prep, which extended from 2008 through June 2012 and involved 19 states that did not receive DELTA funds; and DELTA FOCUS, which extends the work of DELTA and DELTA Prep, and will be funded for the first time in FY2013.

DELTA

The DELTA program was competitively awarded for the first time in 1996, and 14 domestic violence coalitions received funding under the original solicitation. [47] Funding was non- competitively awarded to these 14 coalitions under subsequent grant solicitations through FY2012. The program provided funding and technical assistance to the coalitions to support local efforts to carry out prevention strategies and work at the state level to oversee these strategies. Local prevention efforts were referred to as coordinated community responses (CCRs). The CCRs were led by domestic violence organizations and other stakeholders across multiple sectors, including law enforcement, public health, and faith-based organizations. The coalitions funded CCRs, and provided training and technical assistance to assist CCRs with building their capacity to implement and evaluate primary prevention strategies. For example, the Michigan Coalition Against Domestic and Sexual Violence supported two CCRs—the Arab Community Center for Economic and Social Services and the Lakeshore Alliance Against Domestic and Sexual Violence— that focused on faith-based initiatives. Both CCRs held forums that provided resources and information about the roles of faith leaders in preventing the first-time occurrence of domestic violence. According to the CDC, the forums heightened the focus of faith leaders on healthy and respectful relationships in their premarital counseling activities and at congregational events.

Each of the 14 state coalitions also developed partnerships across their respective states with multiple stakeholders to provide technical assistance to their partners. For example, coalitions worked closely with their state public health agencies. The Kansas Coalition Against Sexual and Domestic Violence partnered with the state public health agency to expand the CDC's Choose Respect Campaign, which encourages healthy relationships for youth. Other state coalitions, such as the Delaware Coalition Against Domestic Violence and the North Carolina Coalition Against Domestic Violence, partnered with the public school system to provide curricula on dating and domestic violence for students.

The 14 state domestic violence coalitions developed five-to-eight year domestic violence prevention plans known as Intimate Partner Violence Prevention Plans. These plans were developed with multiple stakeholders, and they discuss the strategies needed to prevent first-time perpetration or victimization and to build the capacity to implement these strategies. The coalitions are in the process of implementing and evaluating their plans. In addition, the CDC is evaluating the work of the coalitions and the local CCRs to assess changes in the capacity for the states and localities to prevent domestic violence and the impact of each CCR's effort to prevent domestic violence.[48]

DELTA Prep

DELTA Prep was a project that extended from 2008 through June 2012, and was a collaborative effort between the CDC, the CDC Foundation, and the Robert Wood Johnson Foundation.[49] Through DELTA Prep, CDC has extended the DELTA Program to 19 states[50] that were not receiving DELTA funds. State and community leaders in these other states received training and assistance in building prevention strategies, based on the work of the 14 state domestic violence coalitions that receive DELTA funds. DELTA Prep states are integrating primary prevention strategies into their work and the work of their partners, and building leadership for domestic violence prevention in their states.

DELTA FOCUS[51]

DELTA FOCUS continues the work of DELTA and DELTA Prep by providing funding to states and communities for implementation and evaluation of strategies to prevent domestic violence. Like DELTA, the funding will be directed to state domestic violence coalitions to identify and support CCRs that are already engaging in, or have the capacity to engage in, strategies to prevent domestic violence. In addition, state domestic violence coalitions will help the CCRs create a community action plan (CAP) to guide the implementation and evaluation of their strategies and to carry out the CAP, with a focus on "creating and supporting a social environment that allows and promotes equitable and non-violent personal relationships." This program will be funded for the first time in FY2013; funds have not yet been awarded.

CHILDREN AND YOUTH EXPOSED TO DOMESTIC VIOLENCE

Background

FVPSA references, but does not define, children exposed to domestic violence.[52] According to the research literature, this exposure can include children who see and/or hear violent acts, are present for the aftermath (e.g., seeing bruises on a mother's body, moving to a shelter), or live in a house where domestic violence occurs, regardless of whether they see and/or hear the violence. In addition, young people may be exposed to violence in their dating relationships.[53]

FVPSA references the definition of dating violence that is in VAWA, which means violence committed by a person who is or has been in a social relationship of a romantic or intimate nature with the victim, and where the existence of the relationship is determined based on the length, type, and frequency of interaction between the persons in the relationship.[54]

Estimates of children exposed to adult domestic violence and teen dating violence vary based on the definition of these terms and methodology. A frequently cited estimate is that between 10% and 20% of children (approximately 7 million to 10 million children) are exposed to adult domestic violence each year.[55]

Researchers have separately estimated that 20% to 30% of teenagers are exposed to verbal or psychological abuse and 9% are exposed to physical violence by their intimate partners each year.[56] The literature about the impact of domestic violence is evolving. The effects of domestic violence on children can range from little or no effect to severe psychological harm and physical effects, depending on the type and severity of abuse and protective factors, among other variables.[57]

Multiple FVPSA programs are intended to provide support for children exposed to family and related violence:

- One of the purposes of the formula grant program for states is to provide specialized services (i.e., counseling, advocacy, and other assistance) for these children.[58]
- The National Resource Center on Domestic Violence is directed to offer domestic violence programs and research that include both victims and their children exposed to domestic violence.
- The national resource center that addresses mental health and trauma issues is required to address victims of domestic violence and their children who are exposed to this violence.
- State domestic violence coalitions must, among other activities— work with the legal system, child protective services, and children's advocates to develop appropriate responses to child custody and visitation issues in cases involving children exposed to domestic violence.

In addition to these provisions, the FVPSA statute authorizes, and HHS funds, a program for specialized services for abused parents and their children. FVPSA activities for children exposed to domestic violence have also been funded through discretionary funding and funding leveraged through a semipostal stamp.

SPECIALIZED SERVICES FOR ABUSED PARENTS AND THEIR CHILDREN/EXPANDING SERVICES FOR CHILDREN AND YOUTH EXPOSED TO DOMESTIC VIOLENCE[59]

Since 2003, FVPSA has specified that funding must be set aside for activities to address children exposed to domestic violence if the appropriation for shelter, victim services, and program support exceeds $130 million.[60] Under current law, if funding is triggered, HHS must first reserve not less than 25% of funding above $130 million to make grants to a local agency, nonprofit organization, or tribal organization with a demonstrated record of serving victims of domestic violence and their children. These funds are intended to expand the capacity of service programs and community-based programs to prevent future domestic violence by addressing the needs of children exposed to domestic violence.

In FY2010, funding for shelter and services was just over $130 million. HHS reserved the excess funding as well as FVPSA discretionary funding (under shelter, victim services, and program support) to fund specialized services for children through an initiative known as Expanding Services for Children and Youth Exposed to Domestic Violence. HHS also used discretionary money to fund the initiative in FY2011 and FY2012. Total funding for the initiative was $2.5 million. This funding was awarded to five grantees—four state domestic violence coalitions and one national technical assistance provider—to expand supports to children, youth, and parents exposed to domestic violence and build strategies for serving this population.[61] For example, the Alaska Network on Domestic Violence and Sexual Assault used the funding to address the lack of coordination between domestic violence agencies and the child welfare system. Their work involved development of an integrated training curriculum and policies, and creation of a multi- disciplinary team of child welfare and domestic violence stakeholders in four communities.

Support for Runaway and Homeless Youth Demonstration Grant

From FY2007 through FY2009, HHS used FVPSA discretionary funding (through shelter, victim services, and program support) to support eight grantees[62] that received funding through the Runaway and Homeless Youth program. [63] The FVPSA discretionary funds assisted grantees with developing services for runaway and homeless youth experiencing or at risk of experiencing dating violence. The initiative was created because many runaway and homeless youth are believed to come from homes where domestic violence occurs and they may be at risk of abusing their partners or becoming victims of abuse. The initiative funded projects carried out by faith-based and charitable organizations that advocated or provided direct services to runaway and homeless youth or victims of domestic violence. The grants funded training for staff at these organizations to enable them to assist youth in preventing dating violence. The initiative resulted in the development of an online toolkit for advocates in the runaway and homeless youth and domestic and sexual assault fields to help programs better address relationship violence with runaway and homeless youth.[64]

Enhanced Services for Children Who Have Been Exposed to Domestic Violence Semipostal Stamp

The Stamp Out Domestic Violence Act of 2001 (P.L. 107-67) directed the U.S. Postal Service (USPS) to issue a semipostal stamp[65] (between January 1, 2004 and December 31, 2006) to fund services for domestic violence, and to transfer funding from USPS to HHS. HHS designated the Administration for Children and Families (ACF) to administer the stamp act funds. The sale of the semipostal stamp generated $3.2 million. From FY2005 through FY2007, HHS used this revenue to provide FVPSA programming for nine states and local communities[66] to identify, design, and test approaches for providing enhanced direct services for children whose parents were victims of domestic violence. With the funds, grantees (1) expanded the capacity of domestic violence programs to address the needs of children and youth coming into emergency shelters; (2) expanded the capacity of these programs to address the needs of families not in shelters; and (3) developed and enhanced community-based interventions for children exposed to domestic violence whose parents had not sought services or support from a domestic violence program. For example, the Virginia Sexual and Domestic Violence Coalition provided new and enhanced services to over 1,000 children and over 100 parents. In addition, approximately 300 public school personnel received comprehensive training on the impact of exposure to violence on children and youth and how to effectively respond to their needs, among other activities.[67]

FVPSA INTERACTION WITH OTHER FEDERAL LAWS

Apart from CAPTA, FVPSA has been reauthorized by the Violence Against Women Act (VAWA) and shares some of that law's purposes. In addition, FVPSA interacts with the Victims of Crime Act (VOCA) because some FVPSA-funded programs receive VOCA funding to provide legal and other assistance to victims.[68] Further, FVPSA includes provisions that encourage or require HHS to coordinate FVPSA programs with related programs and research carried out by other federal agencies.

Child Abuse and Neglect

FVPSA does not focus on child abuse per se; however, in enacting FVPSA as part of the 1984 amendments to the Child Abuse Prevention and Treatment Act (CAPTA), Members of Congress and other stakeholders noted that child abuse and neglect and intimate partner violence are not isolated problems, and can arise simultaneously.[69] Recent research has focused on this association. In a national study of children in families who come into contact with a public child welfare agency through an investigation of child abuse and neglect, investigative caseworkers identified 28% of the children's caregivers as having a history of domestic violence (against the caregiver) and 12% of those caregivers as being in active domestic violence situations. Further, about 1 out of 10 of the child cases of maltreatment reported included domestic violence. [70]

CAPTA provides funding to states to improve their child protective services (CPS) systems. It requires states, as a condition of receiving certain CAPTA funds, to describe their policies to enhance and promote collaboration between child protective service and domestic violence agencies, among other social service providers.[71] Other federal efforts also address the association between domestic violence and child abuse. For example, the Family Connections Grants program, under Title IV-B of the Social Security Act, provides funding to public child welfare agencies and nonprofit private organizations to help children—whether they are in foster care or at-risk of entering foster care—connect (or reconnect) with birth parents or other extended kin. The funds must be used to establish or support certain activities, including family group-decision making meetings that enable families to develop plans that nurture children and protect them from abuse and neglect, and, when appropriate, to safely facilitate connecting children exposed to domestic violence to relevant services and reconnecting them with the abused parent.[72]

A separate federal program—Maternal, Infant, and Early Childhood Home Visiting Programs— supports efforts to improve the outcomes of young children living in communities with concentrations of domestic violence or child maltreatment, among other factors. The program provides grants to states, territories, and tribes for the support of evidence-based early childhood home visiting programs that provide in-home visits by health or social service professionals with at-risk families.[73]

In addition, HHS and the Department of Justice supported the Greenbook Initiative in the early 2000s. The Greenbook was developed from the efforts of the National Council of Juvenile and Family Court Judges,[74] which convened family court judges and experts on child maltreatment and domestic violence. In 1999, this group developed guidelines for child welfare agencies, domestic violence providers, and dependency courts in responding to domestic violence and child abuse in a publication that came to be known as the Greenbook. Soon after, HHS and DOJ funded efforts in six communities to address domestic violence and child maltreatment by implementing guidelines from the Greenbook.[75] More recently, the Interagency Working Group on Child Abuse and Neglect has convened the Domestic Violence and Children Subcommittee of the Interagency Work Group on Child Abuse and Neglect, which is co-chaired by the director of the FVPSA program.[76]

Violence against Women Act (VAWA)

FVPSA has twice been amended by the Violence Against Women Act (VAWA). Both FVPSA and VAWA are the primary vehicles for federal support to prevent and respond to domestic violence, including children and youth who are exposed to this violence; however, FVPSA has a more singular focus on prevention and services for victims, while VAWA's unique contributions are more focused on law enforcement and legal response to domestic violence.

VAWA was enacted in 1994 after Congress held a series of hearings on the causes and effects of domestic and other forms of violence against women. Members of Congress and others asserted that communities needed a more comprehensive response to violence against women generally— not just against intimate partners—and that perpetrators should face harsher penalties.[77] The shortfalls of legal response and the need for a change in attitudes toward violence against women were primary reasons cited for the passage of VAWA. Since the enactment of VAWA, the federal response to domestic violence has expanded to involve multiple departments and activities that include investigating and prosecuting crimes, providing additional services to victims and abusers, and educating the criminal justice system and other stakeholders about violence against women.

Although VAWA also addresses other forms of violence against women and provides a broader response to domestic violence, some VAWA programs have a similar purpose to those carried out under FVPSA. Congress currently funds VAWA grant programs that address the needs of victims of domestic violence. These programs also provide support to victims of sexual assault, dating violence, and stalking. For example, like the FVPSA grant program for states/territories and tribes, VAWA's STOP (Services, Training, Officers, Prosecutors) Violence Against Women Formula Grant program provides services to victims of domestic/dating violence (and sexual assault and stalking) that include victim advocacy designed to help victims obtain needed resources or services, crisis intervention, and advocacy in navigating the criminal and/or civil legal system.[78] Congress appropriated $189 million for the STOP program in FY2012. Of STOP funds appropriated, 30% must be allocated to victim services. STOP grants also support activities that are not funded under FVPSA, including for law enforcement, courts, and prosecution efforts. Another VAWA program, Transitional Housing Assistance Grants for Victims of Domestic Violence, provides transitional housing services for victims, with the goal of moving them into permanent housing.[79] Congress appropriated $25 million to the program in FY2012. Through the grant program to states/territories and tribes, FVPSA provides emergency shelter to victims of domestic violence and authorizes service providers to assist with locating and securing safe and affordable permanent housing and homelessness prevention services. Both programs are administered by the Department of Justice's Office of Violence Against Women (OVW).

Victims of Crime Act (VOCA)

FVPSA requires that entities receiving funds under the grant programs for states/territories and tribes use a certain share of funding for selected activities, including assistance in accessing other federal and state financial assistance programs. One source of federal finance assistance for victims of domestic violence is the Crime Victims Fund (CVP), authorized under the Victims of Crime Act (VOCA) and administered by the Department of Justice's Office of Victims of Crime (OVC). Within the CVF, funds are available for victims of domestic violence through the Victim Compensation Formula Grants program and Victims Assistance Formula Grants program. The Victims Compensation Grants may be used to reimburse victims of crime for out-of-pocket expenses such as medical and mental health counseling expenses, lost wages, funeral and burial costs, and other costs (except property loss) authorized in a state's compensation statute. In recent years, approximately 40% of all claims filed were for victims of domestic violence. The Victims Assistance Formula Grants may be used to provide grants to state crime victim assistance programs to administer funds for state and community-based victim service program operations. The grants support direct services to victims of crime including information and referral services, crisis counseling, temporary housing, criminal justice advocacy support, and other assistance needs. In recent years, approximately 45% to 50% of victims served by these grants were victims of domestic violence.[80]

FEDERAL COORDINATION

Both FVPSA, which is administered within HHS, and VAWA, which is largely administered within DOJ, require federal agencies to coordinate their efforts to respond to domestic violence. For example, FVPSA authorizes the HHS Secretary to coordinate programs within HHS and to "seek to coordinate" those programs "with programs administered by other federal agencies, that involve or affect efforts to prevent family violence, domestic violence, and dating violence or the provision of assistance for adults and youth victims of family violence, domestic violence, or dating violence."[81] In addition, FVPSA directs HHS to assign employees to coordinate research efforts on family and related violence within HHS and research carried out by other federal agencies.[82]

Similarly, VAWA requires the Attorney General to consult with stakeholders in establishing a task force—comprised of representatives from relevant federal agencies—to coordinate research on domestic violence and to report to Congress on any overlapping or duplication of efforts on domestic violence issues.[83]

In 1995, HHS and DOJ convened the first meeting of the National Advisory Council on Violence Against Women. The purpose of the council was to promote greater awareness on violence against women and to advise the federal government on domestic violence issues. Since that time, the two departments have convened subsequent committees to carry out similar work. In 2010, Attorney General Eric Holder re-chartered the National Advisory Committee on Violence Against Women, which had previously been established in 2006 under his predecessor.[84] As stated in the charter, the committee is intended to provide the Attorney General and the HHS Secretary with policy advice on improving the nation's response to violence against women and coordinating stakeholders at the federal, state, and local levels in this response, with a focus on identifying and implementing successful interventions for children and teens who witness and/or are victimized by intimate partner and sexual violence.

Separately, the director for FVPSA programs and the deputy director of HHS's Office on Women's Health provide leadership to the HHS Steering Committee on Violence Against Women.[85] This committee supports collaborative efforts to address violence against women and their children, and includes representatives from the CDC and other HHS agencies. The members of the committee have established links with professional societies in the health and social service fields to increase attention on women's health and violence issues.

In addition to these collaborative activities, multiple federal agencies participate in the Teen Dating Violence Workgroup, which has met regularly since September 2006 to share information and coordinate teen dating violence program, policy, and research activities to combat teen dating violence from a public health perspective. The workgroup has funded a project to incorporate adolescents in the process for developing a research agenda to address teen dating violence.[86] Finally, the Office of the Vice President coordinates federal efforts to end violence against women, including by convening cabinet-level officials to address issues concerning domestic and other forms of violence against women.[87]

APPENDIX A. DEFINITIONS

Table A-1. Definitions of Family Violence and Related Terms

Term	Definition
"Family Violence:" FVPSA defines this term at 42 U.S.C. §10402(4).	Any act or threatened act of violence, including any forceful detention of an individual, that (1) results or threatens to result in physical injury; and (2) is committed by a person against another individual (including an elderly individual) to or with whom such person is related by blood, is or was related to by marriage, or was otherwise legally related to, or is or was lawfully residing with.
"Domestic Violence:" FVPSA references the definition under the Violence Against Women Act (VAWA), as amended, at 42 U.S.C. §134925(a)(6).	Felony or misdemeanor crimes of violence committed by a current or former spouse of the victim, by a person with whom the victim shares a child in common, by a person who is cohabiting with or has cohabitated with the victim as a spouse, by a person similarly situated to a spouse of the victim under the domestic or family violence laws of the jurisdiction receiving grant monies, or by any other person against an adult or youth victim who is protected from that person's act under the domestic or family violence laws of the jurisdiction.
"Dating Violence:" FVPSA references the definition under VAWA, as amended, at 42 U.S.C. §134925(a)(8).	Violence committed by a person who has been in a social relationship of a romantic or intimate nature with the victim; and where the existence of such a relationship is determined based on consideration of the length of the relationship, the type of relationship, and the frequency of interaction between the persons involved.
"Elder abuse:" FVPSA references this term, but does not point to a specific definition. The term is defined under VAWA, as amended, at 42 U.S.C. §134925(a)(8).	Any action against a person who is 50 years of age or older that constitutes the willful infliction of injury, unreasonable confinement, intimidation, or cruel punishment with resulting physical harm, pain, or mental anguish; or deprivation by a person, including a caregiver, of goods or services with intent to cause physical harm, mental anguish, or mental illness.

Term	Definition
"Child abuse:" FVPSA references this term, but does not point to a specific definition. The term is defined under the Child Abuse Prevention and Treatment Act (CAPTA), at 42 U.S.C. §5101 note.	At a minimum, any recent act or failure to act on the part of a parent or caretaker, which results in death, serious physical or emotional harm, sexual abuse or exploitation, or an act or failure to act that presents an imminent risk of serious harm.
"Witness Domestic Violence:" FVPSA references this term, but does not point to a specific definition. The term is defined in an unrelated context under the Elementary and Secondary Education Act (ESEA) for a program designed to combat the impact of experiencing or witnessing domestic violence for elementary and secondary school children (20 U.S.C. §7275).	To directly observe or be within earshot of an act of domestic violence that constitutes actual or attempted physical assault; a threat or other action that places the victim in fear of domestic violence; or the aftermath of these acts. (The term references an outdated statute that defines "domestic violence" (42 U.S.C. §3796gg-2) under VAWA. This term is now defined at 42 U.S.C. §134925(a)(6).)
"Stalking:" FVPSA references this term, but does not point to a specific definition. The term is defined under VAWA, as amended, at 42 U.S.C. §134925(a)(24).	Engaging in a course of conduct directed at a specific person that would cause a reasonable person to (1) fear for his or her safety or the safety of others; or (2) suffer substantial emotional distress.
"Sexual assault:" FVPSA references this term, but does not point to a specific definition. The term is defined under VAWA, as amended, at 42 U.S.C. §134925(a)(23).	Any sexual abuse or aggregative sexual abuse (as proscribed under18 U.S.C. §§2241 et seq.), whether or not the conduct occurs in the special maritime and territorial jurisdiction of the United States or in a federal prison and includes both assaults committed by offenders who are strangers to the victim and assaults committed by offenders who are known or related by blood or marriage to the victim.

Source: Congressional Research Service (CRS).

APPENDIX B. RESEARCH ON PREVALENCE AND EFFECTS OF DOMESTIC VIOLENCE, THE NEED FOR SHELTER AND SERVICES

Table B-1. Lifetime and 12-Month Prevalence of Violence Committed by an Intimate Partner

National Intimate Partner and Sexual Violence Survey, 2010

	Lifetime		Past 12 Months	
	Weighted Percentage	Estimated Number	Weighted Percentage	Estimated Number
Women				
Rape[a]	9.4%	11,162,000	0.6%	686,000
Physical Violence[b]	32.9%	39,167,000	4.0%	4,741,000
Stalking	2.1%	2,427,000	0.5%	519,000
Rape, Physical Violence, and/or Stalking	35.6%	42,420,000	5.9%	3,53,000
Other Sexual Violence[a]	16.9%	18,973,000	2.3%	2,747,000
Psychological Aggression[c]	48.4%	57,613,000	13.9%	16,578,000
Men				
Rape	N/A	N/A	N/A	N/A
Physical Violence[b]	28.2%	31,893,000	4.7%	5,365,000
Stalking	2.1%	2,427,000	0.5%	519,000
Rape, Physical Violence, and/or Stalking	28.5%	32,280,000	5.0%	5,691,000
Other Sexual Violence[a]	8.0%	9,050,000	2.5%	2,793,000
Psychological Aggression[c]	48.8%	55,249,000	18.1%	20,548,000

Source: U.S. Department of Health and Human Services, Centers for Disease Control and Prevention, National Center for Injury Prevention and Control, *National Intimate Partner and Sexual Violence Survey, 2010 Summary Report*, November 2011, Tables 4.1, 4.2, 4.5, 4.6, 4.7, and 4.8; and Figures 4.3 and 4.4.

Notes: N/A means the estimate is not reported due to the high standard error or small sample size. Intimate partners include cohabiting or non-cohabiting romantic or sexual partners who are opposite or same sex couples. For purposes of the survey, rape is defined as any completed or attempted unwanted vaginal (for women), or anal penetration through the use of physical force or threats of physical harm and includes times when the victim was drunk, high, drugged, or passed out and unable to consent. Physical violence is defined as a range of behaviors from slapping, pushing, or shoving to severe acts such as being beaten, burned, or choked. Stalking is defined as a pattern of harassing or threatening tactics used by a perpetrator that is both unwanted and causes fear of safety concerns in the victim. Other sexual violence includes that the victim was made to penetrate or sexually coerced; or experience unwanted sexual contact or unwanted non-contact sexual experiences. Psychological aggression encompasses both expressive aggression (i.e., the perpetrator acted in a way that seemed dangerous; the victim was told they were a loser, a failure, or not good enough) and coercive control (e.g., the perpetrator tried to keep the victim from seeing or talking to family or friends; the perpetrator made threats to physically harm the victim).

a. The most prevalent type of sexual violence among women over their lifetime was sexual coercion (9.8%) and rape (9.4%), and over the past 12 months was sexual coercion (1.7%). The most prevalent type of sexual violence among males over their lifetime and over the past 12 months was sexual coercion (4.2% and 1.0%, respectively). Sexual coercion means victims were pressured in a non-physical way to have sexual relations (e.g., threatening to end the relationship). Certain other estimates of sexual violence for women and men were not reported due to high standard error or small sample size.

b. The most prevalent type of physical violence among women over their lifetime and the past 12 months was being pushed or shoved (27.5% and 3.4%, respectively), slapped (20.4% and 1.6%, respectively), or slammed against something (17.2% and 1.5%, respectively). The most prevalent type of physical violence among males over their lifetime and the past 12 months was being pushed or shoved (19.4% and 3.8%, respectively), slapped (18.3% and 2.7%, respectively), and hit with a fist or something hard (9.4% and 1.4%, respectively).

c. Among female victims, the most prevalent type of psychological aggression over their lifetimes was being called names like ugly, fat, crazy, or stupid (64.3%); tracked by where they were and what they were doing (61.7%); and insulted, humiliated, or made fun of (58.0%). Among male victims, the most prevalent type of psychological aggression over their lifetimes was being tracked by where they were and what they were doing (63.1%); called names like ugly, fat, crazy, or stupid (51.6%); and insulted, humiliated, or made fun of (58.0%).

Surveys of Domestic Violence Victims Receiving Shelter and Supportive Services

One-Day Census

The majority of FVPSA funds are dedicated to shelter and services. The National Network to End Domestic Violence, an advocacy and support organization for state domestic violence coalitions, conducts a one-day census of domestic violence programs across the country. This count is conducted in September of each year. In 2011, the one-day census of 1,726 domestic violence programs (88.9% of all programs) [88] identified 67,339 victims and their children (41,468 victims and 25,871 children) who were in emergency shelters or transitional housing[89] and/or receiving non-residential assistance and services.[90] The greatest share of children and adults received non-residential services (46%), followed by emergency shelter (35%) and transitional housing (19%). The one-day census also found that domestic violence programs provided the following services: support or advocacy for victims (98%), support or advocacy for children (79%), emergency shelter (74%), transportation (53%), court and legal advocacy (53%), group support and advocacy (48%), advocacy related to housing and landlords (42%), transitional housing (35%), advocacy by a bilingual advocate (33%), financial skills and budgeting assistance (28%), and job training and employment assistance (22%). Victims made 10,581 requests for services on the census day that could not be provided because programs did not have the resources to offer these services. More than 6,700 of these requests were made for emergency shelter and transitional housing. Other unmet service requests sought help with transportation, child care, and legal representation. The reasons the requested services could not be provided include that there was not enough staff (43%) and not enough specialized services (19%), among others.

Surveys of Domestic Violence Shelter and Service Providers

In addition to the one-day census, the U.S. Departments of Health and Human Services and Justice carried out studies in 2009 and 2011 that examined the characteristics of domestic violence shelters and service providers, and the use and need for shelter and services. The studies found that shelters and service providers offered a variety of services, including counseling, parenting classes, case management, and assistance with obtaining protective or restraining orders. The survey of the service providers inquired about funding sources, and the majority of providers indicated they received funding through the Family Violence Prevention and Services Act (FVPSA). A majority also received funding from other federal sources to address domestic violence. Overall, survivors reported that they benefited greatly from these supports, although some continued to have multiple needs.

The 2009 study surveyed 215 shelter programs across eight states and 3,410 shelter residents in those programs.[91] The study examined the characteristics of shelters, the needs of survivors, and whether shelters met their needs, among other topics. On average, these shelters had a capacity of 25 and each had sheltered an average of 130 adults and 114 children over the previous year. The median limit for length of stay was 60 days. Some shelters limited stays to 30 days while others allowed stays up to two years. Shelters reported offering a range of services, including support groups (97%), crisis counseling (96%), individual counseling (92%), parenting classes (55%), counseling for children (54%), and child care (50%). Respondents completed a written survey around the time that they both entered and exited the shelter. Nearly all (99.6%) were female.[92] Approximately one-quarter had first heard of the shelter within a day or two of arriving at it, which likely reflected that they came to the shelter in a crisis situation. Most (70%) respondents were between ages 25 and 50, about 20% were under age 25, and 10% were age 50 and older.[93] Approximately 60% of respondents were mothers. Participants stayed in the shelter for 33 days on average.

The survey asked about 38 different possible needs at both entry and exit. At entry, the most common needs they identified were safety (85%), affordable housing (85%), and learning about their options (80%). At exit, the most common needs identified were personal safety (98%), learning about options (98%), and understanding domestic violence (97%). Most respondents reported that they received the help they wanted across the most common needs; however, not all respondents reported receiving all the help they needed. For example, 70% of those who wanted help with learning about their options received all of the help they needed; 26% received some help and 4% received no help. Survivors were asked to describe what they would have done if they did not have access to a shelter. Many responded that they would have (1) been homeless and may have returned to the abuser because of the need for financial support; (2) lost valuables, jobs, and their children; (3) acted out of desperation, including resorting to violence against their offenders; or (4) continued to remain with their abusive partner.

The 2011 study included 1,467 survivors of domestic violence who received non-residential services at 90 domestic violence programs in four states and at culturally specific programs from across the country.[94] The purpose of the study was to learn more about the characteristics of domestic violence programs, the extent to which services met their expectations, and survivors' assessments of immediate outcomes associated with services. The programs had been in existence for an average of 23 years, had an average staff size of 16, and offered support to between 26 and 8,519 survivors in 2010. Nearly 40% were independent domestic violence programs and about one-quarter were dual domestic violence and sexual assault programs; the rest were part of a larger social service or community agency. Some programs reported whether they received FVPSA funding (65%) and other federal funding under the Victims of Crime Act (73%) or the Violence Against Women Act (76%).[95] The greatest share of services included support groups

(94%), crisis counseling (93%), case management (92%), and help with obtaining protective or restraining orders (88%). The referrals most likely to be made to outside entities were long-term housing (84%), disability issues (80%), and health care (80%).

Respondents were surveyed after having at least two contacts with the program. Most of the respondents were female (95%), with the greatest share of respondents being white (39%). More than half (53.1%) were ages 31 to 50, about one-quarter were ages 21 to 30; and about 10% were under age 21 and 12% were over the age of 50. Nearly half (46%) reported that they came to the United States from another country.[96] Survivors were most likely to report that they wanted help with talking to someone who understood their situation (98%), support to make decisions and changes in their lives (94%), and information about who to call or where to get help (94%), among other needs. For every need, the majority of survivors received all of the help they wanted. Among those who wanted a certain type of help and could not get it, the highest percentage wanted assistance with learning to drive; 29% got none of the help they wanted with driving. Survivors generally reported that they were satisfied with the services received (with most services being ranked as helpful or very helpful). Nine out of ten respondents reported that as a result of the services they received, they felt more hopeful, knew ways to plan for their safety, felt they would achieve their goals, and knew about their rights and options.

APPENDIX C. FUNDING FOR SELECTED FVPSA ACTIVITIES

Table C-1. FVPSA Formula Grant Funding for Services and Shelter for States and Territories, FY2011 and FY2012

State/Territory	FY2011	FY2012
Alabama	$1,495,414	$1,505,670
Alaska	732,822	734,015
Arizona	1,854,261	1,806,120
Arkansas	1,149,461	1,150,209
California	7,628,674	7,629,510
Colorado	1,555,512	1,548,967
Connecticut	1,269,042	1,274,402
Delaware	768,316	769,433
District of Columbia	714,031	713,540

State/Territory	FY2011	FY2012
Florida	4,125,202	4,147,650
Georgia	2,469,135	2,427,979
Hawaii	846,293	856,677
Idaho	893,951	895,790
Illinois	3,055,059	3,021,033
Indiana	1,821,427	1,823,439
Iowa	1,171,978	1,174,822
Kansas	1,136,016	1,138,359
Kentucky	1,420,377	1,418,802
Louisiana	1,454,219	1,455,409
Maine	850,690	850,651
Maryland	1,683,820	1,689,421
Massachusetts	1,853,844	1,835,483
Michigan	2,495,855	2,464,960
Minnesota	1,601,430	1,600,806
Mississippi	1,161,355	1,159,904
Missouri	1,738,605	1,730,060
Montana	785,405	786,694
Nebraska	941,647	944,615
Nevada	1,102,612	1,109,571
New Hampshire	851,883	848,407
New Jersey	2,255,874	2,258,957
New Mexico	982,161	988,550
New York	4,316,026	4,256,486
North Carolina	2,383,880	2,399,266
North Dakota	723,005	726,912
Ohio	2,794,963	2,776,842
Oklahoma	1,301,134	1,307,849
Oregon	1,327,492	1,322,892
Pennsylvania	2,996,938	2,996,833
Rhode Island	800,279	798,611
South Carolina	1,467,371	1,472,767
South Dakota	754,484	753,629
Tennessee	1,797,303	1,797,457
Texas	5,312,632	5,344,757
Utah	1,129,518	1,121,522
Vermont	718,235	718,072
Virginia	2,098,963	2,109,726
Washington	1,867,271	1,868,864
West Virginia	946,051	949,644
Wisconsin	1,675,319	1,673,087
Wyoming	703,499	706,352
Total States	*88,980,734*	*88,861,473*

Table C-1. (Continued)

State/Territory	FY2011	FY2012
American Samoa	129,792	129,547
Guam	129,792	129,547
Northern Mariana Islands	129,792	129,547
Puerto Rico	1,354,424	1,303,025
Virgin Islands	129,792	129,547
Total Territories	*1,873,592*	*1,821,213*
Total	**$90,854,326**	**$90,682,686**

Source: Provided by the U.S. Department of Health and Human Services, Administration for Children and Families, Administration on Children, Youth and Families, Family and Youth Services Bureau, September 2012.

Note: Funding is appropriated to multiple tribal entities. Total funding for tribal entities was $12,979,190 in FY2011 and $12,931,071 in FY2012. Funding by Indian tribe and Alaska Native Village is available for FY2007 and FY2008 at U.S. Department of Health and Human Services, Administration for Children and Families, Administration on Children, Youth and Families, Family and Youth Services Bureau, *Report to Congress FY2007 and FY2008: Family Violence Prevention and Services Program*, Appendix B, http://www.acf.hhs.gov/sites/default/files/fysb/fvpsa2007_2008.pdf.

Table C-2. National and Special Issue Resource Centers Funded Under FVPSA, FY2012

Center	Description	FY2012 Appropriation
National Resource Centers		
National Resource Center on Domestic Violence (NRCDV)	NRCDV provides training and technical assistance to a variety of stakeholders; develops and disseminates information packets that address a range of domestic violence issues; and publishes innovative intervention and model prevention practices, protocols, and policies. NRCDV also operates VAWnet, an online resource center (with support from the Centers for Disease Control and Prevention). NRCDV's Women of Color Network builds the capacity of women of color advocates and activists responding to domestic violence in their communities. NRCDV is operated by an organization of the same name, in Pennsylvania. The website is http://www.nrcdv.org/.	$1,680,000
National Indian Resource Center Addressing Domestic Violence and Safety for Indian Women	The National Indian Resource Center assists tribes and tribal organizations in responding to domestic violence. The resource center is engaged in public awareness, training and technical assistance, policy development, and research activities. The resource center also provides leadership on holding offenders accountable and ensuring that Native women and their children are safe from	$1,250,000

Center	Description	FY2012 Appropriation
(National Indian Resource Center)	violence in their homes and their communities. The resource center is operated by the National Indigenous Women's Resource Center, in Montana. The website is http://www.niwrc.org/.	
Special Issue Resource Centers		
Battered Women's Justice Project (BWJP): Criminal and Civil Justice Center[a]	BWJP provides training to enhance local efforts at coordinating the response of the criminal justice system to domestic violence cases. Training also focuses on improving battered women's access to civil justice options and quality legal representation in civil court proceedings and advocacy for victims of domestic violence by military personnel, among other topics. BWJP is operated by an organization of the same name, in Minnesota. The website is http://www.bwjp.org.	$1,000,000
National Health Resource Center on Domestic Violence (HRC)	HRC supports health care practitioners, administrators and systems, domestic violence experts, survivors, and policy makers at all levels as they improve health care's response to domestic violence. The HRC supports health care leaders through groundbreaking models, education and response programs, advocacy, and technical assistance. The HRC offers free culturally competent materials and in-person trainings that are appropriate for a variety of public and private health professions, settings, and departments. The HRC is operated by Futures Without Violence in California, and the website is http://www.futureswithoutviolence.org/.	$1,000,000
Resource Center on Domestic Violence: Child Protection and Custody (Resource Center)	The Resource Center provides leadership and assistance to consumers and professionals dealing with the issue of child protection and custody in the context of domestic violence. The Resource Center provides information products to those working in the fields of domestic violence, child protection, and custody; and technical assistance, training, policy development, and other resources that are intended to increase the safety, promote stability, and enhance the well- being of battered parents and their children. The Resource Center is operated by the National Council of Juvenile and Family Court Judges in Nevada. The website is http://www.ncjfcj.org/content/view/129/250/.	$1,100,000
National Center on Domestic Violence, Trauma & Mental Health	The National Center on Domestic Violence, Trauma & Mental Health focuses on efforts to (1) promote dialogue between domestic violence and mental health organizations, policy makers, and survivor/advocacy groups about the complex intersections of domestic violence, trauma, and mental health and current strategies to enhance work in this area, (2) build capacity among local agencies, state domestic violence coalitions, and state mental health systems, and (3) provide recommendations on policies, practices, and collaborative models that will positively impact the lives of survivors and their children, particularly in relation to trauma and mental health. The center is operated by an organization of the same name, in Illinois. The website is http://www.nationalcenterdvtraumamh.org.	$1,100,000

Table C-2. (Continued)

Center	Description	FY2012 Appropriation
Special Issue Resource Centers: Culturally Specific Institutes		
Asian and Pacific Islander Institute on Domestic Violence (API Institute)	The Asian and Pacific Islander Institute on Domestic Violence is a national training and technical assistance provider and a clearinghouse on gender violence in Asian, Native Hawaiian, and Pacific Islander communities. It serves a national network of stakeholders working to eliminate violence against women. The API Institute's strategic agenda for programs, communities, and systems focuses on analyzing the issues that inform prevention and intervention on violence against women. This is achieved by improving the cultural relevancy of services; providing the tools to confront and change gender norms; and conducting research and policy reviews that increase access to systems. The API Institute is operated by an organization of the same name, in California. The website is http://www.apiidv.org.	$600,000
Casa de Esperanza	Casa de Esperanza seeks to advance effective responses to eliminate violence and promote healthy relationships within Latina families and communities by increasing access for Latinos experiencing domestic violence through training and technical assistance; producing culturally relevant tools for advocates and practitioners; conducting culturally relevant research that explores the context in which Latino families experience violence; and interjecting the lived realities of Latinas into policy efforts to better support Latino families. Casa de Esperanza is operated by an organization of the same name, in Minnesota. The website is https://www.casadeesperanza.org/.	$600,000
Institute on Domestic Violence in the African American Community (IDVAAC)	IDVAAC is an organization focused on the unique circumstances and life experiences of African Americans as they seek resources and remedies related to the victimization and perpetration of domestic violence in their community. IDVAAC recognizes the impact and high correlation of intimate partner violence to child abuse, elder maltreatment, and community violence. IDVAAC seeks to enhance society's understanding of and ability to end violence in the African American community. IDVAAC is operated by the University of Minnesota. The website is http://www.idvaac.org/index.html.	$600,000
Total		$9,030,000

Source: Congressional Research Service (CRS), based on a review of the center websites and the National Resource Center on Domestic Violence, http://www.VAWnet.org. Funding information from U.S. Department of Health and Human Services, Administration for Children and Families, Administration on Children, Youth and Families, Family and Youth Services Bureau, November 2012.

a. The National Clearinghouse for the Defense of Battered Women is a sub-grantee of the Battered Women's Justice Project. The National Clearinghouse provides technical assistance (but not direct representation) to battered women charged with crimes and to members of their defense team. Most frequently, these cases involve women who have defended themselves against life-threatening violence by their abuser and have been charged with assault or homicide. Some cases involve women coerced into crime by their abuser and charged with "failing to protect" their children from their abuser's violence or charged with "parental kidnapping" after fleeing to protect themselves or their children from their abuser.

End Notes

[1] For further information, see CRS Report R42499, *The Violence Against Women Act: Overview, Legislation, and Federal Funding*, by Lisa N. Sacco.

[2] 42 U.S.C. §10402(4) (Definitions).

[3] This term is sometimes used interchangeably with the word "survivors."

[4] Roger J.R. Levesque, *Culture and Violence: Fostering Change Through Human Rights Law* (Washington, DC: American Psychological Association, 2001), p. 13.

[5] For further information, see CRS Report RL34121, *Child Welfare: Recent and Proposed Federal Funding*, by Emilie Stoltzfus.

[6] For further information, see CRS Report RL33880, *Funding for the Older Americans Act and Other Administration on Aging Programs*, by Angela Napili and Kirsten J. Colello; and U.S. Department of Justice, Office on Women's Health, *Overview of Violence Against Women Activities 2010-2011,* http://www.womenshealth.gov/publications/ federal-reports/OneDepartment-VAW-2010-2011.pdf.

[7] For further information, see CRS Report 94-953, *Social Services Block Grant: Background and Funding* , by Karen E. Lynch.

[8] Rachel Jewkes, "Intimate Partner Violence: Causes and Prevention," *The Lancet*, vol. 359 (April 20, 2002), pp. 1423- 1429.

[9] U.S. Department of Justice, Office of Justice Programs, National Institute of Justice, "Causes and Consequences of Intimate Partner Violence," http://www.nij.gov/nij/topics/crime/ intimate-partner-violence/causes.htm#block.

[10] Phyllis Sharps et al., "Risky Mix: Drinking, Drug Use, and Homicide," *NIJ Journal*, no. 250 (November 2003), https://www.ncjrs.gov/pdffiles1/jr000250d.pdf. The abused women studied were between ages 18 and 50 years old and were romantically or sexually involved with the perpetrator at some time during the past two years. A woman was categorized as abused if she had been physically assaulted, threatened with serious violence, or stalked by a current or former intimate partner.

[11] Michele C. Black et al., *The National Intimate Partner and Sexual Violence Survey: 2010 Summary* Report, U.S. Department of Health and Human Services, National Centers for Disease Control and Prevention, http://www.cdc.gov/ViolencePrevention/pdf/ NISVS_Report2010-a.pdf.

[12] Ibid. The NISVS is a national random telephone survey of the non-institutionalized English and/or Spanish-speaking U.S. population age 18 and older. The study is coordinated by the Centers for Disease Control and Prevention, and developed and fielded with support from the Department of Justice and Department of Defense. Terms such as physical violence and stalking are defined in the report.

[13] Intimate partners may include cohabiting or non-cohabiting romantic or sexual partners and opposite or same sex couples. See **Appendix B** for further definitions.

[14] These terms are defined at U.S. Department of Justice, Office of Justice Programs, Bureau of Justice Statistics, "All Terms and Definitions," http://bjs.ojp.usdoj.gov/index.cfm?ty=tda.

[15] U.S. Department of Justice, Federal Bureau of Investigation, *National Crime Victimization Survey, 2010*, Table 5, September 2011, http://www.bjs.gov/content/pub/pdf/cv10.pdf.

[16] Callie Marie Rennison and Sarah Welchans, U.S. Department of Justice, Office of Justice Programs, Bureau of Justice Statistics, *Intimate Partner Violence*, Special Report, May 2000, http://bjs.ojp.usdoj.gov/content/pub/pdf/ ipv.pdf.

[17] Sandra Naylor Goodwin, Daniel Chandler, and Joan Meisel, *Violence Against Women: The Role of Welfare Reform*, California Institute for Mental Health for the U.S. Department of Justice, April 11, 2003, https://www.ncjrs.gov/ pdffiles1/nij/grants/205792.pdf.

[18] Ola W. Barnett, Cindy L. Miller-Perrin, and Robin D. Perrin, *Family Violence Across the Life Span*, 3rd ed. (Thousand Oaks, CA: Sage Publications, 2011), pp. 14-15. (Hereinafter, Ola W. Barnett, Cindy L. Miller-Perrin, and Robin D. Perrin, *Family Violence Across the Life Span*.)

[19] Susan Schechter, *Women and Male Violence: The Visions and Struggles of the Battered Women's Movement* (Boston: South End Press, 1982), pp. 12-20. (Hereinafter Susan Schechter, *Women and Male Violence: The Visions and Struggles of the Battered Women's Movement*.)

[20] Ola W. Barnett, Cindy L. Miller-Perrin, and Robin D. Perrin, *Family Violence Across the Life Span*, p. 15.

[21] Susan Schechter, *Women and Male Violence: The Visions and Struggles of the Battered Women's Movement*.

[22] Albert B. Roberts, *Sheltering Battered Women: A National Study and Service Guide* (New York: Springer Publishing Company, 1981), pp. 7-11.

[23] Jane O'Reilly, Barbara B. Dolan, and Elizabeth Taylor, "Wife Beating: The Silent Crime," *Time*, September 5, 1983.

[24] U.S. Department of Justice, Office of Justice Programs, Office on Violence Against Women, *The History of the Violence Against Women Act*, http://www.ovw.usdoj.gov/docs/history

[25] CAPTA was originally enacted in 1974 (P.L. 93-247) to create a federal focus for responding to child abuse and neglect and authorize support for training and technical assistance to improve child protective services.

[26] From FY1986 through FY1994, funding for these grants was transferred from HHS to the Department of Justice, which carried out the grants under the Office for Victims of Crime (OVC). DOJ funded 23 projects to train law enforcement officers on domestic violence policies and response procedures, with approximately 16,000 law enforcement officers and other justice system personnel from 25 states receiving this training. The training emphasized officers as participants working with other agencies, victims, and community groups in a coordinated response to a crime problem. U.S. Department of Justice, Office of Justice Programs, Office for Victims of Crime, *Report to Congress*, July 1996, https://www.ncjrs.gov/ovc_archives/repcong/welcome.html and Lisa C. Newmark, Adele V. Harrell, and William Adams, *Evaluation of Police Training Conducted Under the Family Violence Prevention and Services Act*, Urban Institute, June 26, 1995.

[27] The Violence Against Women Act (VAWA) authorizes funding for training and support of law enforcement officials under the Services, Training, Officers, and Prosecutors (STOP) Grant program. For further information, see CRS Report R42499, *The Violence Against Women Act: Overview, Legislation, and Federal Funding*, by Lisa N. Sacco. FVPSA requires state domestic violence coalitions—a statewide nongovernmental nonprofit domestic violence organization comprised primarily of domestic service providers—to work with law enforcement agencies.

[28] 42 U.S.C. §10405 (Allotment of funds).

[29] U.S. Department of Health and Human Services, Administration for Children and Families, Administration on Children, Youth & Families, Family and Youth Services Bureau, "Tribal Domestic Violence Services, 2011."

[30] 42 U.S.C. §10407 (State application).

[31] 42 U.S.C. §10408(b) (Subgrants and uses of funds).

[32] For example, of the 70% set-aside for shelter and supportive services, all of it could be used for shelter; however, an additional 25% must be used for supportive services.

[33] Appendix B provides information from a survey of domestic violence shelters of the types of services provided. Not all of these shelters received FVPSA funding when they were surveyed.

[34] Tribes do not necessarily have domestic violence coalitions and therefore related provisions do not apply; however, as discussed below, state domestic violence coalitions must collaborate with Indian tribes and tribal organizations (and corresponding Native Hawaiian groups or communities) to address the needs of Indian (including Alaska Native) and Native Hawaiian victims of domestic violence. 42 U.S.C. §10411(d)(8). The Violence Against Women Act authorizes funding for tribal domestic violence coalitions under the Tribal Domestic Violence and Sexual Assault Coalitions Grant (42 U.S.C. §3796gg-1). The program is funded by statutory set-asides from the VAWA-authorized STOP program and Sexual Assault Services program.

[35] 42 U.S.C. §10406(c) (Formula grants to states-grant conditions).

[36] 42 U.S.C. §10406(c) (Formula grants to states-grant conditions) and 42 §10408(d) (Subgrants and use of funds- conditions).

[37] 42 U.S.C. §10411 (Grants to State Domestic Violence Coalitions).

[38] SDVCs may include representatives of Indian tribes and tribal organizations. §42 U.S.C. 10411(h).

[39] A SDVC is not required to use funds for certain purposes (i.e., working with judicial and law enforcement agencies, family law judges, criminal court judges, child protective service agencies, and children's advocates) if it receives funding to carry out these activities authorized under the Violence Against Women Act. These activities include grants to help states, state and local courts, state domestic violence coalitions, and other entities develop and strengthen effective law enforcement and prosecution strategies to combat violent crimes against women and develop and strengthen victim services. See 42 U.S.C. §3796gg et seq. and 42 U.S.C. §3796gg(c).

[40] This is based on correspondence with the U.S. Department of Health and Human Services, Administration for Children and Families, Administration on Children, Youth and Families, Family and Youth Services Bureau, September 2012.

[41] 42 U.S.C §10413 (National Domestic Violence Hotline Grant).

[42] The National Council on Family Violence is a nonprofit organization and receives funding from multiple federal, state, and private sources. For further information, see National Council on Family Violence, "About the Hotline," http://www.thehotline.org/about-support/.

[43] Based on correspondence with the U.S. Department of Health and Human Services, Administration for Children and Families, Administration on Children, Youth and Families, Family and Youth Services Bureau, November 2012.

[44] U.S. Department of Health and Human Services, *Administration for Children and Families FY2013 Justification of Estimates for Appropriations Committees.*

[45] 42 U.S.C. §10414. U.S. Department of Health and Human Services, Centers for Disease Control and Prevention, *The Delta Program: Preventing Intimate Partner Violence in the United States,* http://www.cdc.gov/violenceprevention/ pdf/DELTA_AAG-a.pdf; and U.S. Department of Health and Human Services, Centers for Disease Control and Prevention, "Domestic Violence Prevention Enhancement and Leadership Through Alliances (DELTA)," http://www.cdc.gov/violenceprevention/delta/index.html.

[46] Primary prevention strategies attempt to stop both first-time perpetration and victimization by responding to the various factors that influence domestic violence, including (1) individual-level influences (e.g., attitudes and beliefs that support domestic violence, isolation, and a family history of violence), (2) relationship-level influences (e.g., relationships with peers, intimate partners, and families), (3) the community (e.g., social relationships in schools, workplaces, and neighborhoods), and society (e.g., larger, macro-level factors such as

gender inequality, religious or cultural belief systems, or economic or social policies that influence domestic violence). For example, prevention strategies that target individual-level influences are often designed to promote attitudes, beliefs, and behaviors that support intimate partnerships based on mutual respect and trust, such as through education and life skills training. Further, strategies that target community-level influences can be designed to affect the climate and policies in a given system, such as through social marketing campaigns.

[47] These states include AK, CA, DE, FL, KS, MI, MT, NC, ND, NY, OH, RI, VA, and WI.

[48] The CDC has contracted with outside evaluators to assess the state prevention plans and local CCR progress reports, and this evaluation is forthcoming. U.S. Department of Health and Human Services, Centers for Disease Control and Prevention, September 2012.

[49] The CDC Foundation is a nonprofit organization established by Congress that creates programs in partnership with the CDC for fighting threats to health. The Robert Wood Johnson Foundation is a philanthropic organization that focuses on public health issues.

[50] These states include AL, CT, DC, ID, IA, IN, KY, MA, MN, MI, NE, NH, NJ, OK, OR, PA, SC, TX, and WA.

[51] This information is based on correspondence with the U.S. Department of Health and Human Services, Centers for Disease Control and Prevention, November 2012; and U.S. Department of Health and Human Services, Centers for Disease Control and Prevention, "Funding Opportunity, DELETA FOCUS (Domestic Violence Prevention Enhancement Leadership Through Alliances, Focusing on Outcomes for Communities United with States)."

[52] A separate federal program authorized under the Elementary and Secondary Education (ESEA) defines "witnessing domestic violence" for purposes of a program whose purpose is to combat the impact of experiencing or witnessing this violence by elementary and secondary school children. Under this program, witnessing domestic violence refers to directly observing or being within earshot of an act of domestic violence that constitutes actual or attempted physical assault; a threat or other action that places the victim in fear of domestic violence; or the aftermath of these acts. See 20 U.S.C. §7275. The program has not been funded. The statute references an outdated statute that defines "domestic violence" (42 U.S.C. §3796gg-2) under VAWA. This term is now defined at 42 U.S.C. §134925(a)(6)).

[53] Jeffrey J. Edleson, Narae Shin, and Katy K. Armedariz Johnson, "Measuring Children's Exposure to Domestic Violence: The Development and Testing of the Child Exposure to Domestic Violence (CEDV) Scale," *Children and Youth Services Review*, vol. 30, November 6, 2007, p. 502-521. (Hereinafter Jeffrey J. Edleson, Narae Shin, and Katy K. Armedariz Johnson, "Measuring Children's Exposure to Domestic Violence: The Development and Testing of the Child Exposure to Domestic Violence (CEDV) Scale.")

[54] 42 U.S.C. §13925(a)(8).

[55] Jeffrey J. Edleson, Narae Shin, and Katy K. Armedariz Johnson, "Measuring Children's Exposure to Domestic Violence: The Development and Testing of the Child Exposure to Domestic Violence (CEDV) Scale."

[56] Carrie Mulford and Peggy Giordano, *Teen Dating Violence: A Closer Look at Adolescent Romantic Relationships*, U.S. Department of Justice, National Institute for Justice, October 27, 2008, http://www.nij.gov/journals/261/teen- dating-violence.htm#note2; and U.S. Department of Health and Human Services; Centers for Disease Control and Prevention, *Youth Risk Behavior Surveillance System, 2011 Results*, http://www.cdc.gov/healthyyouth/yrbs/index.htm.

[57] Alice Summers, *Children's Exposure to Domestic Violence: A Guide to Research and Resources*, National Council of Juvenile and Family Court Judges and U.S. Department of Justice, Office of Justice Programs, Office of Juvenile Justice and Delinquency Prevention, 2006, pp. 5-6, http://www.safestartcenter.org/pdf/childrensexpostoviolence.pdf.

[58] In the 2011 one-day census count of domestic violence shelter and service providers, nearly 80% reported providing services and advocacy for children. See, National Network to End

Domestic Violence (NNEDV), *Domestic Violence Counts 2011*, http://nnedv.org/docs/Census

[59] 42 U.S.C. §10406.

[60] This was enacted as a provision under the Keeping Children and Families Safe Act of 2003 (P.L. 108-36). The 2010 reauthorization of FVPSA (P.L. 111-320) created a new section, specialized services for abused parents and their children, which has the same purpose as the original provision.

[61] The grantees were New Jersey Coalition for Battered Women, Wisconsin Coalition Against Domestic Violence, Alaska Network on Domestic Violence and Sexual Assault, Idaho Coalition Against Sexual and Domestic Violence, and Family Violence Prevention Fund. For further information, see http://www.acf.hhs.gov/programs/fysb/content/familyviolence/discretionary.htm.

[62] The grantees were Council of Churches of Greater Bridgeport, Bridgeport, CT; Youth In Need, St. Charles, MO; Texas Network of Youth Services, Austin, TX; Hoyleton Youth & Family Services, Washington Park, IL; Family Violence Prevention Center, Raleigh, NC; Youth Services of Tulsa, OK; LUK Crisis Center, Inc., Fitchburg, MA; and Center for Community Solutions, San Diego, CA.

[63] For further information about this population and HHS' Runaway and Homeless Youth program, see CRS Report RL33785, *Runaway and Homeless Youth: Demographics and Programs*, by Adrienne L. Fernandes-Alcantara.

[64] U.S. Department of Health and Human Services, "Runaway & Homeless Youth and Relationship Violence Toolkit," http://www.nrcdv.org/rhydvtoolkit/index.html.

[65] For further information about semipostal stamps, see CRS Report RS22611, *Common Questions About Postage and Stamps*, by Kevin R. Kosar.

[66] The grantees were East Bay Community Foundation in Oakland, CA; Women's Crisis and Family Outreach Center in Castle Rock, CO; District of Columbia Department of Human Services in Washington, DC; Department of Human Services in Lansing, MI; New York State Coalition Against Domestic Violence in Albany, NY; Oklahoma Coalition Against Domestic Violence and Sexual Assault in Oklahoma City, OK; Womenspace, Inc. in Eugene, OR; Pennsylvania Coalition Against Domestic Violence in Harrisburg, PA; and Virginia Sexual and Domestic Violence Action Alliance in Richmond, VA. For further information about the projects, see U.S. Department of Health and Human Services, Administration for Children and Families, Administration on Children, Youth, and Families, Family and Youth Services Bureau, *Family Violence Semipostal Stamp: Enhancing Services for Children and Youth Who Are Exposed to Domestic Violence, Report to Congress,* 2008, http://www.acf.hhs.gov/programs/fysb/content/docs/ fv_stamp_08.pdf.

[67] U.S. Department of Health and Human Services, Administration for Children and Families, Administration on Children, Youth, and Families, Family and Youth Services Bureau, *Family Violence Prevention and Services Program, Report to Congress FY2007-FY2008*, http://www.acf.hhs.gov/programs/fysb/content/docs/fvpsa2007-2008.pdf.

[68] The majority of non-residential domestic violence programs participating in a 2011 survey reported that they received FVPSA funding (65%) and other federal funding under the Victims of Crime Act (73%) or the Violence Against Women Act (76%). FVPSA funding made up 18.0% of the programs' budget; VOCA funding made up 21.0% of the programs' budget; and VAWA funding made up 14.6% of the programs' budget. Eleanor Lynn, Jill Bradshaw, and Anne Menard, *Meeting Survivors' Needs Through Non-Residential Domestic Violence Services & Supports: Results of a Multi-State Study*, University of Connecticut, School of Social Work and National Resource Center on Domestic Violence, prepared for the U.S. Department of Justice, National Institute of Justice, November 2011, http://www.vawnet.org/Assoc_Files_VAWnet/DVServicesStudy-FINALReport2011.pdf.

[69] U.S. Congress, House Select Committee on Children, Youth, and Families, *Violence and Abuse in American Families*, 98th Cong., 2nd sess., June 14, 1984. See for example, statement of Congressman David Marriott.

[70] Cecilia Casanueva et al., *NSCAW II Baseline Report: Maltreatment*, U.S. Department of Health and Human Services, Administration for Children and Families, Office of Planning, Research and Evaluation, Final Report, August 2011, pp. 5-6, 15, http://www.acf.hhs.gov/programs/opre/abuse_neglect/nscaw/reports/nscaw2_maltreatment/nscaw2_maltreatment.pdf. Those percentages include all children without regard to whether the child was subsequently removed from the home. For children who stayed in the home following the investigation, the comparable percentages were the same (28% and 12%); for children removed from the home following the investigation, the comparable numbers were slightly higher (30% and 16%); however, this percentage difference was not statistically significant. The study did not compare the prevalence of domestic violence for families generally. The 2010 National Intimate Partner and Sexual Violence Survey (NISVS), discussed in this report, found that more than one-third (35.6%) of women experienced rape, physical violence, and/or stalking in their lifetime and 5.9% experienced them in the past year.

[71] 42 U.S.C. §5106a(a)(14).

[72] 42 U.SC. §627.

[73] For further information, see CRS Report R42428, *The Maternal and Child Health Services Block Grant: Background and Funding*, by Amalia K. Corby-Edwards.

[74] 42 U.SC. §627. The National Council of Juvenile and Family Court Judges is the operator of the FVPSA-funded Child Protection and Custody Resource Center.

[75] For further information, see National Council of Juvenile and Family Court Judges, "The Greenbook Initiative," http://www.thegreenbook.info/contact_us.htm.

[76] U.S. Department of Health and Human Services and Office on Women's Health, *Overview of Violence Against Women Activities 2010-2011*, http://www.womenshealth.gov/publications/federal-reports/OneDepartment-VAW-2010- 2011.pdf.

[77] In their introduction to the Violence Against Women Act, then-Senator Joseph Biden and Senator Barbara Boxer highlighted the weak legal response to violence against women by police and prosecutors. Senators Biden and Boxer, "Violence Against Women," Remarks in the Senate, *Congressional Record*, June 21, 1994. See also Joseph Biden, "Violence Against Women: The Congressional Response," *American Psychologist*, vol. 48, no. 10 (October 1993), pp. 1059-1061; Barbara Vobejda, "Battered Women's Cry Relayed Up From Grass Roots," *Washington Post*, July 6, 1994, p. A1.

[78] University of Southern Maine, Muskie School of Public Service, *STOP Formula Grant Program*, http://muskie.usm.maine.edu/vawamei/stopformulagraphs.htm.

[79] The 2000 reauthorization of VAWA (P.L. 106-386) authorized the program and codified it under the FVPSA statute (Chapter 110 of Title 42). The law directed the HHS Secretary to award grants to provide assistance to individuals fleeing a situation of domestic violence who are homeless or in need of transitional housing (and their dependents) and for whom emergency shelter services are unavailable or insufficient. This program remained part of the FVPSA chapter until it was struck by the FVPSA reauthorization law in 2010 (P.L. 111-320). Separately, the Prosecutorial Remedies and Other Tools to End the Exploitation of Children Today Act of 2003 (PROTECT Act, P.L. 108-21) codified the program as part of the VAWA statute (Chapter 136 of Title 42) and directed the Attorney General to award grants to states and other entities to carry out transitional housing programs.

[80] 42 U.S.C. 10408(b)(G)(1). Deposits to the CVF come from criminal finds, forfeited appearance bonds, penalties, and special assessments collected by U.S. Attorneys' Offices, federal courts, and the Federal Bureau of Prisoners. For further information, see CRS Report R42672, *The Crime Victims Fund: Federal Support for Victims of Crime*, by Lisa N. Sacco.

[81] 42 U.S.C. §10404(a)(5).

[82] 42 U.S.C. §10404(b)(3)(C).

[83] 42 U.S.C. §14042(a).

[84] U.S. Department of Justice, "National Advisory Committee on Violence Against Women," http://www.ovw.usdoj.gov/nac.html and "Charge to the National Advisory Committee on

Violence Against Women," April 2006, http://www.justice.gov/archive/ovw/docs/final_nac_charge.pdf.

[85] U.S. Department of Health and Human Services, Office on Women's Health, *Overview of Violence Against Women Activities 2010-2011,* http://www.womenshealth.gov/publications/federal-reports/OneDepartment-VAW-2010- 2011.pdf.

[86] U.S. Department of Justice, Office of Justice Programs, National Institute of Justice, "Setting the Teen Dating Violence Research Agenda," http://www.nij.gov/topics/crime/intimate-partner-violence/teen-dating-violence/research- agenda.htm.

[87] Office of the President, "1 is 2 Many," http://www.whitehouse.gov/1is2many.

[88] The FVPSA grants for states, territories, and tribes funded 1,600 domestic violence shelters and 1,100 non-residential service sites in FY2011; some programs have both shelters and non-residential services. This information was provided by the U.S. Department of Health and Human Services, Administration for Children and Families, Administration on Children, Youth and Families, Family and Youth Services Bureau, September 2012.

[89] The Transitional Housing Assistance Grants for Victims of Domestic Violence is authorized and funded under VAWA. The program directs the Attorney General to award grants to states and other entities to carry out transitional housing programs.

[90] National Network to End Domestic Violence (NNEDV), *Domestic Violence Counts 2011,* http://nnedv.org/docs/   Census/DVCounts2011/DVCounts11_NatlReport_Color.pdf. NNEDV has identified 1,944 local domestic violence programs in the United States.

[91] This included 81% of shelters in the eight states: CT, FL, IL, MI, NM, OK, TN, and WA. Eleanor, Lyon, Shannon Lane, and Anne Menard, University of Connecticut, School of Social Work and National Resource Center on Domestic Violence, *Meeting Survivors' Needs: A Multi-State Study of Domestic Violence Shelter Experiences,* prepared for the U.S. Department of Justice, National Institute of Justice, Final Report, February 2008, https://www.ncjrs.gov/pdffiles1/nij/grants/225025.pdf.

[92] Thirteen of the respondents were men. As noted in the study, most men receive services other than emergency shelter from domestic violence programs, or obtain housing assistance through motel vouchers or safe homes and therefore would not be included in the study.

[93] Approximately 20% were under age 25 and 10% were ages 50 and older.

[94] Eleanor Lynn, Jill Bradshaw, and Anne Menard, *Meeting Survivors' Needs Through Non-Residential Domestic Violence Services & Supports: Results of a Multi-State Study,* University of Connecticut, School of Social Work and National Resource Center on Domestic Violence, prepared for the U.S. Department of Justice, National Institute of Justice, November 2011, http://www.vawnet.org/Assoc_Files_VAWnet/DVServicesStudy-FINALReport2011.pdf.

[95] Less than half of the programs were able to provide data about what percentage of their budget came from specific sources. Of those that responded about FVPSA funding, this funding made up 18.0% of their budget; of those that responded about VOCA funding, this funding made up 21.0% of their budget; and of those responding about VAWA funding, this funding made up 14.6% of their budget.

[96] Though not addressed in the report, the high representation of individuals who came from another country may be due to the oversampling of domestic violence programs that were culturally specific.

In: Federal Responses to Domestic Violence   ISBN: 978-1-62618-951-5
Editor: Sara P. Zimmerman   © 2013 Nova Science Publishers, Inc.

Chapter 2

THE VIOLENCE AGAINST WOMEN ACT: OVERVIEW, LEGISLATION, AND FEDERAL FUNDING*

Lisa N. Sacco

SUMMARY

In 1994, Congress passed the Violence Against Women Act (VAWA, P.L. 103-322). The act was intended to change attitudes toward domestic violence, foster awareness of domestic violence, improve services and provisions for victims, and revise the manner in which the criminal justice system responds to domestic violence and sex crimes. The legislation created new programs within the Departments of Justice and Health and Human Services that aimed to reduce domestic violence and improve response to and recovery from domestic violence incidents. VAWA primarily addresses certain types of violent crime through grant programs to state, tribal, and local governments; nonprofit organizations; and universities. VAWA programs target the crimes of intimate partner violence, dating violence, sexual assault, and stalking.

In 1995, the Office on Violence Against Women (OVW) was created administratively within the Department of Justice to administer federal grants authorized under VAWA. In 2002, Congress codified the OVW as a separate

---

* This is an edited, reformatted and augmented version of the Congressional Research Service Publication, CRS Report for Congress R42499, dated February 19, 2013.

office within the Department of Justice (DOJ). Since its creation, the OVW has awarded more than $4.7 billion in grants. While the OVW administers the majority of VAWA authorized grants, other federal agencies, including the Centers for Disease Control and Prevention and the Office of Justice Programs, also manage VAWA grants.

Since 1994, VAWA has been modified and reauthorized several times. In 2000, Congress reauthorized the programs under VAWA, enhanced federal domestic violence and stalking penalties, added protections for abused foreign nationals, and created programs for elderly and disabled women. In 2005, Congress again reauthorized VAWA. In addition to reauthorizing the programs under VAWA, the legislation enhanced penalties for repeat stalking offenders; added additional protections for battered and trafficked foreign nationals; and created programs for sexual assault victims and American Indian victims of domestic violence and related crimes; and created programs designed to improve the public health response to domestic violence.

Authorization for appropriations for the programs under VAWA expired in 2011. VAWA programs are currently unauthorized; however, programs have continued to receive appropriations. In the 112th Congress, bills (S. 1925 and H.R. 4970) were passed in each chamber that would have reauthorized most of the programs under VAWA, among other things. H.R. 4970 differed in substantive ways from S. 1925, including with respect to the VAWA-related immigration provisions, the authority it would have given Indian tribes to enforce domestic violence and related crimes against non-Indian individuals, and in the populations it would have included under its definition of underserved population. Neither bill was enacted into law. Selected issues with these bills are discussed in **Appendix B**.

In the 113th Congress, two bills (H.R. 11 and S. 47) have been introduced that would reauthorize most of the programs under VAWA, among other things. On February 12, 2013, the Senate passed S. 47 as amended. The Senate amended S. 47 so the bill would amend and authorize appropriations for the Trafficking Victims Protection Act of 2000, enhance measures to combat trafficking in persons, and amend VAWA grant purpose areas to include sex trafficking. Aside from these amendments, S. 47 and H.R. 11 are similar. A description of these bills is provided in this report.

H.R. 11 and S. 47 contain many of the same provisions that were in reauthorization bills from the 112th Congress. These bills would reauthorize most VAWA grant programs and authorize appropriations at a lower level. Like S. 1925, these bills propose new provisions for certain populations such as American Indian tribes. Both bills would grant authority to Indian tribes to enforce domestic violence and related crimes against non-Indian individuals.

H.R. 11 and S. 47 also differ from reauthorization bills from the 112th Congress. The 113th bills include new provisions to address the rape kit backlog by amending the DNA Analysis Backlog Elimination Act of 2000 (P.L. 106-546). As mentioned, S. 47 now includes provisions that would address trafficking in persons. Additionally, some items that *had* been included in reauthorization bills from the 112th Congress are *not* included in H.R. 11 and S. 47, such as the proposal (in S. 1925 only) to temporarily increase the cap on the number of U visas available for abused foreign nationals (from 10,000 to 15,000). These issues and others are discussed in this report.

BACKGROUND AND HISTORY OF THE VIOLENCE AGAINST WOMEN ACT (VAWA)

The Violence Against Women Act (VAWA), currently up for reauthorization, was originally passed by Congress as Title IV of the Violent Crime Control and Law Enforcement Act of 1994 (P.L. 103-322). This act addressed congressional concerns about violent crime, and violence against women in particular, in several ways. Among other things, it enhanced investigations and prosecutions of sex offenses by allowing for enhanced sentencing of repeat federal sex offenders; mandating restitution to victims of specified federal sex offenses; and providing grants to state, local, and tribal law enforcement entities to investigate and prosecute violent crimes against women.

Congressional passage of VAWA was ultimately spurred on by decades of growing unease over the rising violent crime rate and a focus on women as crime victims. Beginning in the 1960s, the violent crime rate rose steadily,[1] igniting concern from both the public and the federal government. Supplementing the concern for the nation's rising violent crime rate was the concern for violence against women. In the 1970s, grassroots organizations began to stress the need for attitudinal change regarding violence against women. These organizations sought a change in attitude among both the public as well as the law enforcement community.[2]

In the 1980s, researchers began to address the violence against women issue as well. For instance, Straus and Gelles collected data on family violence and attributed declines in spousal assault to heightened awareness of the issue by both men and the criminal justice system.[3] The criminal justice system and the public were beginning to view family violence as a crime rather than a private family matter.[4]

In 1984, Congress enacted the Family Violence Prevention and Services Act (FVPSA, P.L. 98-457) to assist states in preventing incidents of family violence and to provide shelter and related assistance to victims of family violence and their dependents. While FVPSA authorized programs similar to those discussed in this report and has reauthorized programs that were originally created by VAWA, such as the National Domestic Violence Hotline, it is a separate piece of legislation and beyond the scope of this report.

In 1994, Congress passed a major crime bill, the Violent Crime Control and Law Enforcement Act of 1994 (P.L. 103-322). Among other things, the bill created an unprecedented number of programs geared toward helping local law enforcement fight violent crime and servicing victims of violent crime. In their introduction to the Violence Against Women Act, then-Senator Joseph Biden and Senator Barbara Boxer highlighted the weak response to violence against women by police and prosecutors.[5] The shortfalls of legal response and the need for a change in attitudes toward violence against women were primary reasons cited for the passage of VAWA.[6]

Since it was enacted in 1994, Congress has twice reauthorized VAWA. The most recent authorization of appropriations for VAWA programs expired in FY2011, however, these programs have continued to receive funding. In the 113th Congress, two bills (H.R. 11, Violence Against Women Reauthorization Act of 2013 and S. 47, Violence Against Women Reauthorization Act of 2013) have been introduced that would reauthorize most of the programs under VAWA, among other things. On February 12, 2013, the Senate passed S. 47 as amended. H.R. 11 and S. 47 are very similar and include new provisions for immigrants and American Indian tribes. These issues and others are discussed in this report.

This report provides a brief legislative history of VAWA and an overview of the crimes addressed through VAWA. **Appendix A** outlines funding information for VAWA authorized programs from FY2008 through FY2012. **Appendix B** provides discussion of selected issues of the VAWA reauthorization bills from the 112th Congress. The report concludes with a brief description of the VAWA reauthorization bills.

VIOLENCE AGAINST WOMEN ACT OF 1994

As mentioned, VAWA was originally passed by Congress as part of the broader Violent Crime Control and Law Enforcement Act of 1994. The Violence Against Women Act of 1994 (1) enhanced investigations and prosecutions of sex offenses and (2) provided for a number of grant programs to address the issue of violence against women from a variety of angles, including law enforcement, public and private entities and service providers, and victims of crime. The sections below highlight examples of these VAWA provisions.

Investigations and Prosecutions

As passed in 1994, VAWA impacted federal investigations and prosecutions of cases involving violence against women in a number of ways. For instance, it established new offenses and penalties for the violation of a protection order as well as stalking in which an abuser crossed a state line to injure or harass another, or forced a victim to cross a state line under duress and then physically harmed the victim in the course of a violent crime. It added new provisions to require states and territories to enforce protection orders issued by other states, tribes, and territories. VAWA also allowed for enhanced sentencing of repeat federal sex offenders. It also authorized funding for the Attorney General to develop training programs to assist probation and parole officers in working with released sex offenders.

In addition, VAWA established a new requirement for pretrial detention in federal sex offense or child pornography felony cases. It also modified the Federal Rules of Evidence to include new procedures specifying that, with few exceptions, a victim's past sexual behavior was not admissible in federal criminal and civil cases of sexual misconduct.[7] In addition, VAWA asked the Attorney General to study measures in place to ensure confidentiality between sexual assault or domestic violence victims and their counselors.

VAWA mandated restitution to victims of specified federal sex offenses, specifically sexual abuse as well as sexual exploitation and other abuse of children. It also established new provisions, including a civil remedy that allows victims of sexual assault to seek civil penalties from their alleged assailants,[8] and a provision that allows rape victims to demand that their alleged assailants be tested for the HIV virus.

Grant Programs

VAWA created a number of grant programs for a range of activities, including programs aimed at (1) preventing domestic violence and related crimes; (2) encouraging collaboration among law enforcement, judicial personnel, and public/private sector providers with respect to services for victims of domestic violence and related crimes; (3) investigating and prosecuting domestic violence and related crimes; and (4) addressing the needs of individuals in a special population group (e.g., elderly, disabled, children and youth, individuals of ethnic and racial communities, and nonimmigrant women). VAWA grants are administered by the Department of Justice, Office on Violence Against Women and Office of Justice Programs as well as by the Department of Health and Human Services, Centers for Disease Control.

Under VAWA, grants were authorized for capital improvements to prevent crime in public transportation systems as well as in public and national parks. It also expanded the Family Violence Prevention and Services Act (FVPSA)[9] to include grants for youth education on domestic violence and intimate partner violence as well as to include grants for community intervention and prevention programs. As mentioned, VAWA provided for federal grants to state, local, and tribal law enforcement entities to investigate and prosecute violent crimes against women. It established an additional grant to bolster investigations and prosecutions in rural areas. It also established a grant program to encourage state, local, and tribal arrest policies in domestic violence cases.

VAWA authorized grants for education and training for judges and court personnel in state and federal courts on the laws of rape, sexual assault, domestic violence, and other crimes of violence motivated by the victim's gender. It also authorized grants to assist state and local governments in entering data on stalking and domestic violence into national databases.

VAWA authorized the expansion of grants under the Public Health Service Act[10] to include rape prevention education. Additionally, it expanded the purposes of the Runaway and Homeless Youth Act[11] to allow for grant funding to assist youth at risk of (or who have been subjected to) sexual abuse. VAWA reauthorized the Court-Appointed Special Advocate Program and the Child Abuse Training Programs for Judicial Personnel and Practitioners. It also authorized funding for Grants for Televised Testimony by Victims of Child Abuse.

VAWA established the National Domestic Violence Hotline and authorized funding for its operation.[12] It also authorized funding for battered women's shelters, in addition to including special protections for battered nonimmigrant women and children.[13]

Other VAWA Requirements

Beyond the criminal justice improvements and grant programs, VAWA included provisions for several other activities, including

- requiring that the U.S. Postal Service take measures to ensure confidentiality of domestic violence shelters and abused persons' addresses;
- mandating federal research by the Attorney General, National Academy of Sciences, and Secretary of Health and Human Services to increase the government's understanding of violence against women; and
- requesting special studies on campus sexual assault and battered women's syndrome.

Office on Violence against Women

In 1995, the Office on Violence Against Women (OVW) was administratively created within the Department of Justice (DOJ) to administer the grants authorized under VAWA.[14] Since its creation, the OVW has awarded more than $4.7 billion in grants and cooperative agreements to state, tribal, and local governments, nonprofit organizations, and universities.[15] While the OVW administers the majority of VAWA authorized grants, other federal agencies, including the Centers for Disease Control and Prevention (CDC) and the Office of Justice Programs (OJP), also manage VAWA funds. See **Table A-1** for an outline of current VAWA authorized grant programs.

Categories of Crime Addressed through VAWA

VAWA grant programs address the needs of victims of domestic violence, sexual assault, dating violence, and stalking. VAWA treats these as distinct crimes which involve a wide range of victim demographics. For domestic violence, sexual assault, and stalking, the risk of victimization is highest for women.[16] For dating violence, the risk of victimization is the same for both men and women.[17] Victimization data on these crimes are available from two national surveys, the National Crime Victimization Survey (NCVS) and the Youth Risk Behavior Surveillance System[18] and the Federal Bureau of Investigation's (FBI's) Uniform Crime Reporting (UCR) Program.[19] UCR data vary from survey data because the UCR describes crimes that were reported to law enforcement while survey data describe self-reported crimes that were not necessarily reported to law enforcement. Due to differences in methodology, survey data are not comparable to UCR data.[20]

Domestic Violence

As discussed, public concern over violence against women prompted the original passage of VAWA. As such, VAWA legislation and programs have historically emphasized women as victims. More recently, however, there has been a focus on ensuring the needs of all victims are met through provisions of VAWA programs.[21] Domestic violence is a complex crime and is often labeled as family violence or intimate partner violence. Under VAWA, domestic violence is generally interpreted as intimate partner violence. Intimate partner violence includes felony or misdemeanor crimes committed by spouses or ex-spouses, boyfriends or girlfriends, and ex-boyfriends or ex-girlfriends. Crimes may include sexual assault, simple or aggravated assault, and homicide. As defined in statute for the purposes of VAWA grant programs, domestic violence includes

> felony or misdemeanor crimes of violence committed by a current or former spouse of the victim, by a person with whom the victim shares a child in common, by a person who is cohabiting with or has cohabitated with the victim as a spouse, by a person similarly situated to a spouse of the victim under the domestic or family violence laws of the jurisdiction receiving grant monies, or by any other person against an adult or youth victim who is protected from that person's acts under the domestic or family violence laws of the jurisdiction.[22]

From 1994 to 2010, the rate of intimate partner violence declined by 64%, and over this 17 year period, approximately four in five victims of intimate partner violence were female.[23] In 2010, there were 407,700 females that reported victimization by an intimate partner (3.1 per 1,000 persons aged 12 and older), compared to 101,530 males (0.8 per 1,000 persons aged 12 and older) who reported victimization by an intimate partner. According to NCVS data, intimate partner victimization rates also vary by age and race. Females aged 18 or older generally experience higher rates of intimate partner violence than females aged 12 to 17. Rates of intimate partner violence have also been historically higher for black females than white females.[24]

In 2010, a survey conducted by the Centers for Disease Control and Prevention included questions about lifetime victimization. The CDC estimates that 24.3% of women (one in four women) and 13.8% of men (one in seven men) have experienced severe physical violence[25] by an intimate partner in their lifetime.[26]

Intimate Partner Homicide

Since peaking in the early 1990s, the violent and property crime rates have declined. Overall homicide rates and intimate partner homicide rates have also declined. Researchers have studied the range of social factors that may influence homicide rates and have suggested possible reasons for the decline in intimate partner homicide rates.

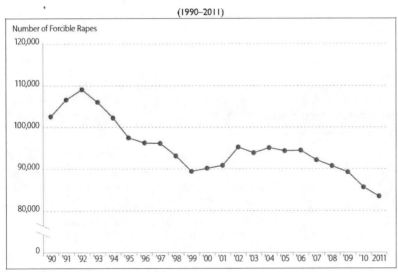

Source: CRS presentation of UCR data. These data are available at http://www.fbi.gov/about-us/cjis/ucr/crime-in-the-u.s/2009 and http://www.fbi.gov/about-us/cjis/ucr/crime-in-the-u.s/2011/crime-in-the-u.s.-2011/tables/table-1.

Note: These data include only female victims; from 1990-2011 the FBI definition of rape did not include male victims.

Figure 1. Forcible Rapes Known to Police.

For instance, most intimate partner homicides involve married couples; as such, some researchers have suggested the decline in marriage rates among young adults as a contributing factor in the decline in intimate partner homicide rates.[27] Additionally, divorce and separation rates have increased. Fewer marriages may result in less exposure to abusive partners and fewer marriages may suggest that those who do marry are more selective in choosing a partner.[28]

Overall, homicide is committed largely by males, mostly victimizing males. From 1980 through 2008, males made up 90% of all offenders and 77% of all homicide victims; however, females were more likely than males to be victims of intimate partner homicide.[29] From 1980 through 2008, female homicide victims were six times more likely than male victims to have been a victim of intimate partner homicide, and 63% of all intimate partner homicide victims were female.[30]

Sexual Assault

While intimate partner violence can, and often does, include sexual assault,[31] it is viewed as a separate category of crime under VAWA. Sexual assault may include the crimes of forcible rape, attempted forcible rape, assault with intent to rape, statutory rape, and other sexual offenses. Sexual assault is not defined in the U.S. Code, but other associated crimes, such as sexual abuse and aggravated sexual abuse, are defined in the U.S. Code.[32] Under VAWA, sexual assault includes any conduct that may be described as sexual abuse or aggravated sexual abuse.

According to statistics from the NCVS, there were 184,390 sexual assaults in 2010.[33] These data are not comprehensive because some victimizations are not reported to law enforcement. Moreover, these data are not comparable to UCR data because the NCVS includes male victims in its definition of sexual assault, and UCR statistics from 2010 do not include male victims.

According to the FBI's UCR Program, 83,425 forcible rapes were reported to law enforcement in 2011. Since 1990, when 102,555 forcible rapes were reported to law enforcement, this figure has fluctuated but has declined overall, as illustrated in **Figure 1**.

Through 2011, the FBI defined forcible rape as, "the carnal knowledge of a female forcibly and against her will."[34] Forcible rape statistics include attempted forcible rape and assault with intent to rape, but exclude statutory rape without force and other sex offenses.[35] In January 2012, the FBI revised its definition of forcible rape to include male victims.[36] Future UCR reports will include rape statistics for male victims.

Dating Violence

Under VAWA, dating violence refers to "violence committed by a person who is or has been in a social relationship of a romantic or intimate nature with the victim."[37] The relationship between the offender and victim is determined based on the following factors: (1) the length of the relationship; (2) the type of relationship; and (3) the frequency of interaction between the persons involved in the relationship.[38]

Reports on dating violence usually refer to teenagers as the relevant age demographic. According to the *2011 Youth Risk Behavior Survey*, approximately 9.4% of high school students had been "hit, slapped, or physically hurt on purpose by their boyfriend or girlfriend" in the past year.[39] Unlike other crimes addressed by VAWA, males were equally likely as females to report this outcome.[40]

Stalking

Stalking is defined as "a course of conduct directed at a specific person that would cause a reasonable person to feel fear."[41] All 50 states, the District of Columbia, and U.S. Territories have enacted anti-stalking laws, and these laws vary in their definition.[42] Federal law makes it unlawful to (1) travel across state lines or use the mail or computer; (2) with the intent to injure or harass another; and (3) as a result, places that person in reasonable fear of death or serious bodily injury or causes substantial emotional distress to that person or a member of that person's family.[43]

According to the NCVS, 3.3 million individuals aged 18 and older were victims of stalking in 2006.[44] Females were at greater risk than males for stalking victimization, and individuals aged 18-24 were at greater risk than those individuals aged 25 or older.[45] According to the CDC, 10.7% of women and 2.1% of men have been stalked by an intimate partner in their lifetime.[46]

Reauthorizations of VAWA

Since it was enacted in 1994, Congress has twice reauthorized VAWA. Of note, both reauthorizations had broad bipartisan support.[47]

- In 2000, Congress reauthorized VAWA through the Victims of Trafficking and Violence Protection Act (P.L. 106-386). Modifications included additional protections for battered nonimmigrants,[48] a new program for victims in need of transitional housing, a requirement for grant recipients to submit reports on the effectiveness of programs, new programs designed to protect elderly and disabled women, mandatory funds to be used exclusively for rape prevention and education programs, and inclusion of victims of dating violence.[49] VAWA 2000 amended interstate stalking and domestic violence law to include (1) a person who travels in interstate or foreign commerce with the intent to kill, injure, harass, or intimidate a spouse or intimate partner, and who in the course of such travel commits or attempts to commit a crime of violence against the spouse or intimate partner; (2) a person who causes a spouse or intimate partner to travel in interstate or foreign commerce by force or coercion and in the course of such travel commits or attempts to commit a crime of violence against the spouse or intimate partner; (3) a person who travels in interstate or foreign commerce with the intent of violating a protection order or causes a person to travel in interstate or foreign commerce by force or coercion and violates a protection order; and (4) a person who uses the mail or any facility of interstate or foreign commerce to engage in a course of conduct that would place a person in reasonable fear of harm to themselves or their immediate family or intimate partner.[50] Also, the act added the intimate partners of victims as people covered under the interstate stalking statute.

- In 2005, Congress reauthorized VAWA through the Violence Against Women and Department of Justice Reauthorization Act (P.L. 109-162).[51] The legislation added protections for battered and trafficked nonimmigrants,[52] enhanced penalties for repeat stalking offenders, added programs for American Indian victims, sexual assault victims and programs designed to improve the public health response to domestic violence. The act emphasized collaboration among law enforcement; health and housing professionals; and women, men, and youth alliances, and encourages community initiatives to address these issues. The act also created the Office of Audit, Assessment and Management (OAAM).

REAUTHORIZATION OF VAWA AND THE 113TH CONGRESS

Authorization for appropriations for the programs under VAWA expired in 2011; however, programs have continued to receive appropriations.[53] In the

112th Congress, bills (S. 1925 and H.R. 4970) were passed in each chamber that would have reauthorized most of the programs under VAWA, among other things. H.R. 4970 differed in substantive ways from S. 1925, including with respect to the VAWA-related immigration provisions, the authority it would have given Indian tribes to enforce domestic violence and related crimes against non-Indian individuals, and in the populations it would have included under its definition of underserved population. Neither bill was enacted into law. Selected issues with these bills are discussed in **Appendix B**.

Two bills have been introduced in the 113th Congress that would reauthorize appropriations for programs under VAWA, among other things. On January 22, 2013, Senator Patrick Leahy introduced the Violence Against Women Act of 2013 (S. 47) and Representative Gwen Moore introduced the Violence Against Women Reauthorization Act of 2013 (H.R. 11). On February 12, 2013, the Senate passed S. 47 as amended. The Senate amended S. 47 so the bill would amend and authorize appropriations for the Trafficking Victims Protection Act of 2000 (Division A of P.L. 106-386), enhance measures to combat trafficking in persons, and amend grant purpose areas to include sex trafficking.[54] Aside from these amendments, S. 47 and H.R. 11 are similar.

H.R. 11 and S. 47 include new provisions for certain populations such as American Indian tribes. Both bills would grant authority to Indian tribes to enforce domestic violence and related crimes against non-Indian individuals. Selected provisions of H.R. 11 and S. 47 are described in this section.

Description of H.R. 11 and S. 47

Both H.R. 11 and S. 47 would, among other things,

- reauthorize most VAWA grant programs and authorize appropriations at a lower level, in general;[55]
- consolidate several VAWA grant programs (42 U.S.C. 14043c through 14043c–3) that address services and education for youth into one grant program entitled Creating Hope through Outreach, Options, Services, and Education for Children and Youth;
- consolidate several VAWA grant programs that support families in the justice system and strengthen the healthcare system's response to domestic violence, dating violence, and stalking;

- repeal four VAWA grant programs (*Interdisciplinary Training and Education on Domestic Violence and Other Types of Violence and Abuse [42 U.S.C. 294H]; Research on Effective Interventions in the Health Care Setting [42 U.S.C. 13973]; Development of Curricula and Pilot Programs for Home Visitation Projects [42 U.S.C. 14043d-3]; Engaging Men and Youth in Preventing Domestic Violence, Dating Violence, Sexual Assault, and Stalking [42 U.S.C. 14043d-4]; and Public Awareness Campaign [42 U.S.C. 14045c);*
- enhance protection of personally identifiable information of victims;[56]
- include victims of dating violence in the Transitional Housing Assistance Grant Program and ensure that victims are not subject to prohibited activities, including background checks or clinical evaluations, to determine eligibility for services;
- promote additional housing rights for victims of domestic violence, dating violence, sexual assault, and stalking, including a provision that states that an applicant may not be denied public housing on the basis that the person has been a victim of domestic violence, dating violence, sexual assault, and stalking;
- redefine "linguistically and culturally specific services" by removing "linguistically" from the term, and amending the definition to address the needs of culturally specific communities;
- with respect to providing VAWA-related services, add the terms "population specific services" and "population specific organizations," which focus on "members of a specific underserved population";[57]
- establish a nondiscrimination provision for all VAWA grant programs to ensure that victims are not denied services on the basis of race, color, religion, national origin, sex, gender identity, sexual orientation, or disability;
- expand the purpose areas of several VAWA grants to address the needs of sexual assault survivors to include strengthening law enforcement and forensic response and urging jurisdictions to evaluate and reduce rape kit backlogs;
- amend the DNA Analysis Backlog Elimination Act of 2000 (P.L. 106-546)[58] to strengthen audit requirements for sexual assault evidence backlogs and require that for each of fiscal years 2014 through 2018, not less than 75% of the total Debbie Smith grant[59] amounts be awarded to carry out DNA analyses of samples from crime scenes for inclusion in the Combined DNA Index System[60] and to increase the

capacity of state or local government laboratories to carry out DNA analyses;

- establish a new requirement that at least 20% of funds within the STOP (Services, Training, Officers, Prosecutors) program and 25% of funds within the Grants to Encourage Arrest Policies and Enforce Protection Orders program be directed to programs that meaningfully address sexual assault;
- define "individual in later life" to mean a person who is 50 years of age or older;
- enhance criminal penalties for assaulting a spouse, intimate partner, or dating partner;[61]
- enhance criminal penalties for criminal and civil rights violations involving sexual abuse;
- expand the purpose areas of grants to tribal governments and coalitions to include sex trafficking;
- amend rules for sexual acts in federal custodial facilities by adding "the commission of a sexual act" as grounds for civil action by a federal prisoner and mandating that detention facilities operated by the Department of Homeland Security and custodial facilities operated by the Department of Health and Human Services adopt national standards set forth through the Prison Rape Elimination Act of 2003 (P.L. 108-79);
- expand the purpose areas of grants for American Indian tribal governments and coalitions to develop and promote legislation and policies that enhance best practices for responding to violent crimes against Indian women and raise awareness of and response to domestic violence to include identifying and providing technical assistance to enhance access to services for Indian women victims of domestic and sexual violence, including sex trafficking;
- redefine "underserved populations" to include those who may be discriminated against based on religion, sexual orientation or gender identity;[62]
- require the Office on Violence Against Women to establish a biennial conferral process with grantees and key stakeholders;[63]
- allow VAWA petition information[64] to be shared with other government agencies for national security purposes, provided the confidentiality provisions of §384(b) of Illegal Immigration Reform and Immigrant Responsibility Act of 1996 are maintained, and permit DOJ to go beyond the record of conviction when determining whether

a crime of domestic violence constitutes a crime of violence when determining whether an individual is deportable;[65]

- establish new mandatory grant guidelines for campuses and universities in their incident response procedures and development of programs to prevent domestic violence, sexual assault, stalking, and dating violence;
- expand the definition of cyberstalking to include use of "any electronic communication device or electronic communication system of interstate commerce;"
- create a voluntary two-year pilot program for Indian tribes that make a request to the Attorney General to be designated as a participating tribe to have *special domestic violence criminal jurisdiction* over such cases (*Note: the provision would provide for dismissal of such cases if the victim and/or defendant are not Indians or do not have sufficient ties to the Indian tribe*);[66]
- grant Indian tribes civil jurisdiction to issue and enforce protection orders over any person;[67] and
- create a new grant program to assist Indian tribes in exercising special criminal jurisdiction over cases involving domestic violence.

In amending S. 47, the Senate bill has provisions that are not part of the House reauthorization bill. In contrast to H.R. 11, S. 47 would

- expand the purpose area for the Creating Hope through Outreach, Options, Services, and Education for Children and Youth grant program[68] to include victims of sex trafficking; and
- amend and authorize appropriations for the Trafficking Victims Protection Act of 2000.[69]

Selected Similarities and Differences in Bills from the 112th Congress

H.R. 11 and S. 47 contain many of the same provisions that were in reauthorization bills from the 112th Congress. These bills would reauthorize most VAWA grant programs and authorize appropriations at a lower level. Like S. 1925, these bills propose new provisions for certain populations such as American Indian tribes. Both bills would grant authority to Indian tribes to enforce domestic violence and related crimes against non-Indian individuals.

Also similar to S. 1925, both bills would establish a nondiscrimination provision for all VAWA grant programs to ensure that victims are not denied services on the basis of race, color, religion, national origin, sex, gender identity, sexual orientation, or disability.

H.R. 11 and S. 47 also differ from reauthorization bills from the 112th Congress. Unlike reauthorization bills from the 112th Congress, H.R. 11 and S. 47 include new provisions to address the rape kit backlog by amending the DNA Analysis Backlog Elimination Act of 2000 (P.L. 106-546). As mentioned, S. 47 now includes provisions that would address trafficking in persons.

Additionally, some items that *had* been included in reauthorization bills from the 112th Congress are *not* included in H.R. 11 and S. 47, such as the proposal (in S. 1925 only) to temporarily increase the cap on the number of U visas available for battered nonimmigrants (from 10,000 to 15,000). Also in contrast to the current reauthorization bills, S. 1925 would have amended the Immigration and Nationality Act to include a third drunk driving offense as an aggravated felony for the purposes of removing a noncitizen from the United States, but H.R. 11 and S. 47 do not propose to do this. Finally, S. 1925 had proposed to amend federal law to include a mandatory minimum sentence for aggravated sexual abuse by force or threat, but H.R. 11 and S. 47 do not propose to do this.

As previously mentioned, selected issues with reauthorization bills from the 112th Congress are discussed in **Appendix B**.

APPENDIX A. FEDERAL PROGRAMS AUTHORIZED BY VAWA

The fundamental goals of VAWA are to prevent violent crime, respond to the needs of crime victims, learn more about violence against women, and change public attitudes about domestic violence. This comprehensive strategy involves a collaborative effort by the criminal justice system, social service agencies, research organizations, public health organizations, and various private organizations. VAWA has supported these efforts primarily through federal grant programs that provide funding to state, tribal, and local governments, nonprofit organizations, and universities. **Table A-1** provides descriptions of VAWA programs. **Table A-2** provides a five-year funding history for these programs.

Table A-1. Descriptions of Current VAWA Authorized Programs under the Department of Justice (DOJ) and Department of Health and Human Services (HHS)

Program and U.S. Code Citation (by Administrative Agency)	Purposes and Goals	Organizations Eligible to Apply
Office on Violence Against Women (DOJ)		
STOP (Services, Training, Officers, and Prosecutors) Grant Program (42 U.S.C. §3796gg and 28 C.F.R. §90)	The purpose of this formula grant program is to enhance advocacy and improve the criminal justice system's response to violent crimes against women.	States and territories.[a]
Grants to Encourage Arrest Policies and Enforcement of Protection Orders (42 U.S.C. §3796hh)	The purpose of this grant program is to encourage state, local, and tribal courts and governments to treat domestic violence, dating violence, stalking, and sexual assault as serious crimes.	States; territories; tribal governments; units of local government; and state, tribal, territorial, and local courts (including juvenile courts).
Civil Legal Assistance for Victims Grant Program (42 U.S.C. §3796gg–6)	The purpose of this grant program is to strengthen civil and criminal legal assistance for victims of sexual assault, stalking, domestic violence, and dating violence through innovative and collaborative programs.	Private, nonprofit organizations; tribal governments and organizations; territorial organizations; and publicly funded organizations not acting in a governmental capacity (e.g., law schools).
Grants to Indian Tribal Governments Program (42 U.S.C. §3796gg–10)	The goals of this grant program are to develop and enhance effective plans for tribal governments to respond to violence committed against American Indian women and improve services for these women; strengthen the tribal criminal justice system; create community education and prevention campaigns; address the needs of children who witness domestic violence; provide supervised visitation and safe exchange programs; and provide transitional housing assistance and legal assistance.	Tribal governments; designees of tribal governments.
Rural Domestic Violence, Dating Violence, Sexual Assault, Stalking, and Child Abuse Enforcement Assistance (42 U.S.C. §13971)	The purpose of these grants is to enhance the safety of victims of domestic violence, dating violence, sexual assault, and stalking by supporting projects uniquely designed to address and prevent these crimes in rural jurisdictions.	States; territories; tribal governments; units of local government; nonprofit, public or private organizations, including tribal organizations.[b]
Transitional Housing Assistance Grants for Victims of Domestic Violence (42 U.S.C. §13975)[c]	The purpose of this grant program is to use a holistic, victim-centered approach to provide transitional housing services for victims of domestic violence, dating violence, sexual assault, and stalking, and to move them into permanent housing.	States; territories; tribal governments; units of local government; domestic violence and sexual assault victim service providers; domestic violence and sexual assault coalitions; and other

Program and U.S. Code Citation (by Administrative Agency)	Purposes and Goals	Organizations Eligible to Apply
		nonprofit, nongovernmental organizations, or community-based and culturally specific organizations.[d]
Sexual Assault Services Program (42 U.S.C. §14043g and 42 U.S.C. §3796gg)	This program encompasses five different funding streams to (1) states and territories, (2) tribes, (3) state sexual assault coalitions, (4) tribal coalitions, and (5) culturally specific organizations. The purpose of these grants is to provide intervention, advocacy, accompaniment, support services, and related assistance for adult, youth, and child victims of sexual assault, family and household members of victims, and those collaterally affected by the sexual assault.	States; territories; tribal governments; state, territorial, and tribal sexual assault coalitions; and private, nonprofit organizations that focus primarily on culturally-specific communities.[e]
Consolidated Youth Oriented Program[f]	This program consolidates four VAWA authorized programs: Engaging Men and Youth in Prevention, Grants to Assist Children and Youth Exposed to Violence, Supporting Teens Through Education Program (STEP), and Services to Advocate and Respond to Youth. This program supports projects that implement one or both of the primary purpose areas: (1) comprehensive child- and youth-centered prevention and intervention projects that maximize community-based efforts and evidence-informed practices to more fully address domestic violence, dating violence, sexual assault and stalking (DDSS); and (2) multi-faceted prevention strategies that involve community organizing, outreach, public education and mobilization that utilize men as influencers of other men and boys and encourages them to work as allies with women and girls to prevent DDSS.	Nonprofit, nongovernmental entities with either (1) a demonstrated primary goal of providing services to children and youth who are victims of and/or exposed to domestic violence, dating violence, sexual assault, or stalking (DDSS), or (2) a primary goal of serving adult victims of DDSS, but have a demonstrated history of providing comprehensive services to children or youth who are victims of and/or exposed to DDSS, or (3) a demonstrated history of creating effective public education and/or community organizing campaigns to encourage men and boys to work as allies with women and girls to prevent DDSS; tribal governments or tribal nonprofit organizations that provide services to children or youth who are victims of and/or exposed to DDSS; and territorial, tribal or unit of local government entities.
Safe Havens: Supervised Visitation and Support Program (42 U.S.C. §10420)[g]	The purpose of this grant program is to provide an opportunity for communities to support the supervised visitation and safe exchange of children in situations involving domestic violence, dating violence, child abuse, sexual assault, or stalking.	States; territories; and tribal governments.

Table A-1. (Continued)

Program and U.S. Code Citation (by Administrative Agency)	Purposes and Goals	Organizations Eligible to Apply
Grants to Reduce Domestic Violence, Dating Violence, Sexual Assault, and Stalking on Campus Program (42 U.S.C. §14045b)	The purpose of this grant is to encourage institutions of higher education to adopt comprehensive, coordinated responses to domestic violence, dating violence, sexual assault, and stalking.	Institutions of higher education.
Education, Training and Services to End Violence Against and Abuse of Women with Disabilities (42 U.S.C. §3796gg–7)	The purpose of this grant program is to build the capacity to address the growing problem of domestic violence, sexual assault, and dating violence against individuals with disabilities.	States; territories; tribal governments or organizations; units of local government; nonprofit, nongovernmental victim service organizations.[h]
Court Training and Improvements (42 U.S.C. §14043 et seq.)	The purpose of this grant is to improve court responses to adult and youth domestic violence, dating violence, sexual assault, and stalking.	Federal, state, tribal, territorial, or local courts or court-based programs; and national, state, tribal, territorial, or local private, nonprofit organizations with demonstrated expertise in developing and providing judicial education about domestic violence, dating violence, sexual assault, or stalking.
Enhanced Training and Service to End Violence and Abuse of Women Later in Life (42 U.S.C. §14041a)	The purpose of this grant program is to provide or enhance training and services for victims of elder abuse, neglect, or exploitation, including victims of domestic violence, dating violence, sexual assault, or stalking.	States; territories; tribal governments or organizations; units of local government; nonprofit, nongovernmental victim service organizations.[i]
Tribal Domestic Violence and Sexual Assault Coalitions Grant (42 U.S.C. §3796gg–1)	The purpose of this grant program is to increase awareness of domestic violence and sexual assault against American Indian and Alaska Native women; enhance the response to violence against women at the tribal, federal, and state levels; and identify and provide technical assistance to coalition membership and tribal communities to enhance access to essential services.	Tribal coalitions; and individuals and organizations proposing to create tribal coalitions.
Grant for National Resource Center on Workplace Responses to Assist Victims of Domestic and Sexual Violence (42 U.S.C. §14043f)	The purpose of this grant program is to provide for the establishment and operation of a national resource center on workplace responses to assist victims of domestic and sexual violence.[j]	Nonprofit organizations; and tribal organizations.

Program and U.S. Code Citation (by Administrative Agency)	Purposes and Goals	Organizations Eligible to Apply
Services to Advocate and Respond to Youth (42 U.S.C. §14043c)	The purpose of this grant program is to fund projects that create and implement programs and services to respond to the needs of youth who are victims of domestic violence, dating violence, sexual assault, or stalking.	Nonprofit, nongovernmental organizations; community-based organizations; tribes; and tribal organizations.[k]
Children and Youth Exposed to Violence (42 U.S.C. §14043d–2)	The purpose of this grant program is to mitigate the effects of domestic violence, dating violence, sexual assault, and stalking on children and youth exposed to violence and reduce the risk of future victimization or perpetration of these crimes.	States; territories; tribal governments; units of local government; nonprofit, victim service organizations; community-based organizations; and tribal organizations.[l]
Engaging Men and Youth in Preventing Domestic Violence, Dating Violence, Sexual Assault, and Stalking (42 U.S.C. §14043d–4)	The purpose of this grant program is to fund projects that develop or enhance efforts to engage men in preventing crimes of domestic violence, dating violence, sexual assault and stalking with the goal of developing mutually respectful, nonviolent relationships.	States; territories; tribal governments; units of local government; nonprofit, nongovernmental domestic violence, dating violence, sexual assault, or stalking victim service providers or coalitions; community-based child or youth service organizations.[m]
Supporting Teens through Education and Protection (STEP) (42 U.S.C. §14043c–3)	The purpose of this grant program is to support projects that provide training to school personnel; develop policies and procedures for response; provide support services; develop effective prevention strategies; and collaborate with mentoring organizations to support middle and high school students who are victims of domestic violence, dating violence, sexual assault, or stalking.	State, local, tribal, and territorial courts; public, private, and military high schools and middle schools.[n]
Grants to Enhance Culturally and Linguistically Specific Services for Victims of Domestic Violence, Dating Violence, Sexual Assault, and Stalking (42 U.S.C. §14045a)	The purpose of this grant program is to (1) promote the maintenance and replication of existing successful domestic violence, dating violence, sexual assault, and stalking community-based programs providing culturally and linguistically specific services and other resources, and (2) support the development of innovative culturally and linguistically specific strategies and projects to enhance access to services and resources for victims of violence against women.	Community-based programs whose primary purpose is providing culturally and linguistically specific services to victims of domestic violence, dating violence, sexual assault, and stalking, and whose primary purpose is providing culturally and linguistically specific services who can partner with a program having demonstrated expertise in serving these victims.

Table A-1. (Continued)

Program and U.S. Code Citation (by Administrative Agency)	Purposes and Goals	Organizations Eligible to Apply
Grants to State Sexual Assault and Domestic Violence Coalitions Program (42 U.S.C. § 3796gg)	The purpose of this grant program is to fund coalitions that provide direct support to member rape crisis centers through funding, training and technical assistance, public awareness, and public policy advocacy.	States and territorial coalitions.
Office of Justice Programs (DOJ)		
Court Appointed Special Advocates for Victims of Child Abuse (42 U.S.C. §13013 et seq.)[o]	The purpose of this grant program is to provide trained individuals who are appointed by judges to advocate for the best interest of children who are involved in the juvenile and family court system due to abuse or neglect.[p]	National organizations.[q]
Training Programs to Assist Probation and Parole Officers (42 U.S.C. §13941)	The purpose of this program is to establish criteria and develop training programs to assist probation and parole officers and other personnel who work with released sex offenders in the areas of case management, supervision, and relapse prevention.	NA
Violence Against Women and Family Research and Evaluation Program (NIJ)[r]	The purpose of this research program is to promote the safety of women and family members, and to increase the efficiency and effectiveness of the criminal justice system's response to these crimes.	NA
Research on Violence Against Indian Women, National Baseline Study (NIJ) (42 U.S.C. §3796gg–10 Note)	The purpose of this program is to examine violence against American Indian and Alaska Native women and identify factors that place this population at risk for victimization; evaluate the effectiveness of federal, state, tribal, and local responses to violence against American Indian and Alaska Native women; and propose recommendations to improve effectiveness of these responses.	NA
National Stalker and Domestic Violence Reduction (42 U.S.C. §14031 et seq.)	The purpose of this program is to improve processes for entering data on stalking and domestic violence into local, state, and national crime information databases.	States; and units of local government.[s]
Tracking of Violence Against Women: National Tribal Sex	The purpose of this program is to develop and maintain a national tribal sex offender registry.	Tribal governments; and tribal organizations.

Program and U.S. Code Citation (by Administrative Agency)	Purposes and Goals	Organizations Eligible to Apply
Offender Registry (28 U.S.C. §534 Note)		
Centers for Disease Control and Prevention (HHS)		
Rape Prevention and Education Grant Program (42 U.S.C. §280b–1b)	The purpose of this program is to is to strengthen sexual violence prevention efforts in the states and territories. The goal is to increase awareness about sexual violence through educational seminars, hotline operations, and development of informational materials.	States and territories.

Sources: Descriptions of grant programs' purposes and goals are taken from statute; the Office on Violence Against Women (OVW), available at http://www.ovw.usdoj.gov/ovwgrantprograms.htm; National Institute of Justice, available at http://www.nij.gov/topics/crime/violence National Resource Center on Workplace Responses, available at http://www.workplacesrespond.org; and the Centers for Disease Control and Prevention (CDC), available at http://www.cdc.gov/ViolencePrevention/RPE/. The organizations eligible to apply for grants are taken from the relevant statute and the *OVW Fiscal Year 2012 Grant Program Solicitation Reference Guide*, available at http://www.ovw.usdoj.gov/docs/resource-guidebook.pdf and from the RPE Grant Program description available at http://www.cdc.gov/ ViolencePrevention/RPE/.

Notes: Programs in this table represent current programs that were authorized by the Violence Against Women and Department of Justice Reauthorization Act of 2005 (VAWA 2005, P.L. 109-162) and A Bill to Make Technical Corrections to the Violence Against Women and Department of Justice Reauthorization Act of 2005 (P.L. 109- 271). Programs that did not receive appropriations in FY2010-FY2012 are not included in this table. Programs that are funded by set-asides from VAWA authorized programs are reflected in this table. See **Table A-2** for an outline of all programs authorized by VAWA 2005.

a. Indian tribal governments, units of local government, and nonprofit, nongovernmental victim service programs may receive sub-grants from states.

b. All applicants must propose to serve a rural area, as defined in statute.

c. This program was originally authorized by the Prosecutorial Remedies and Other Tools to End the Exploitation of Children Today (PROTECT) Act of 2003 (P.L. 108-21), and was reauthorized by the Violence Against Women and Department of Justice Reauthorization Act of 2005.

d. These organizations must have a documented history of effective work concerning domestic violence, dating violence, sexual assault, or stalking to carry out programs to provide assistance to minors, adults, and their dependents who are homeless, or in need of transitional housing or other housing assistance, as a result of fleeing a situation of domestic violence, dating violence, sexual assault, or stalking and for whom emergency shelter services or other crisis intervention services are unavailable or insufficient.

e. These organizations must (1) have documented organizational experience in the area of sexual assault intervention or have entered into a partnership with an organization having such expertise; (2) have expertise in the development of community-based, linguistically and culturally specific outreach and intervention services relevant for the specific communities to whom assistance would be provided or have the capacity to link to existing services in the community tailored to the needs of culturally specific populations; and (3) have an advisory board or steering committee and staffing which is reflective of the targeted culturally specific community.

f. The Consolidated Youth Oriented Program is not defined in statute.

g. This program was originally authorized by the Victims of Trafficking and Violence Protection Act of 2000 (P.L. 106-386). It was modified and reauthorized by the Violence Against Women Reauthorization Act of 2005.

h. Examples of organizations include state domestic violence or sexual assault coalitions and nonprofit, nongovernmental organizations that serve disabled individuals.

i. These organizations must have demonstrated experience in assisting elderly women or demonstrated experience in addressing domestic violence, dating violence, sexual assault, and stalking.

j. This grant currently funds The Workplaces Respond to Domestic and Sexual Violence: A National Resource Center Project. This project offers information to those interested in providing effective workplace responses to victims of domestic violence, sexual violence, dating violence and stalking.

k. Nonprofit, nongovernmental organizations must either (1) have the primary purpose of providing services to teen and young adult victims of domestic violence, dating violence, sexual assault, or stalking or (2) provide services for runaway or homeless youth affected by domestic or sexual abuse. Tribes and tribal organizations must provide services primarily to tribal youth or tribal victims of domestic violence, dating violence, sexual assault or stalking.

l. A state, local, or tribal government is only eligible if it is partnered with an eligible organization. Eligible organizations must have a documented history of effective work concerning children or youth exposed to domestic violence, dating violence, sexual assault, or stalking, including programs that provide culturally specific services, Head Start, childcare, faith-based organizations, after school programs, and health and mental health providers.

m. A state, local, or tribal government is only eligible if it is partnered with an eligible organization or a program that provides culturally specific services. Community- based organizations must have demonstrated experience and expertise in addressing the needs and concerns of young people. Organizations eligible to create public education campaigns and community organizing must have a documented history of creating and administering effective public education campaigns addressing the prevention of domestic violence, dating violence, sexual assault or stalking.

n. Schools are only eligible if they are partnered with (1) a domestic violence victim service provider that has a history of working on domestic violence and the impact that domestic violence and dating violence have on children and youth; and (2) a sexual assault victim service provider, such as a rape crisis center, program serving tribal victims of sexual assault, or coalition or other nonprofit, nongovernmental organization carrying out a community-based sexual assault program, that has a history of effective work concerning sexual assault and the impact that sexual assault has on children and youth. Schools may also partner with a law enforcement agency, courts, organizations and service providers addressing sexual harassment, bullying or gang-related violence in schools, and any other such agencies or organizations with the capacity to provide effective assistance to the adult, youth, and minor victims served by the partnership.

o. This program was originally authorized by the Victims of Child Abuse Act (P.L. 101-647). In 1994, 2000, and 2005, VAWA has reauthorized funding for this program.

p. The National Court Appointed Special Advocate (CASA) Program has received this award each year and makes sub-grants, on a competitive base, to local CASA programs. The CASA Program also provides training and technical assistance. For additional information, see http://www.casaforchildren.org.

q. National organizations must have broad membership among court-appointed special advocates, and must have demonstrated experience in grant administration of court-appointed special advocate programs and in providing training and technical assistance to court-appointed special advocate program. The organization may be may be a local public or nonprofit agency that has demonstrated the willingness to initiate, sustain, and expand a court-appointed special advocate program.

r. This program is not authorized by VAWA. It is included in this table because it is funded by a set-aside from the STOP Program.

s. States and local units of government must certify that it has or intends to establish a program that enters into the National Crime Information Center records of warrants, arrests, convictions and protection orders.

Table A-2. FY2008-FY2012 Authorization and Appropriations for VAWA Programs
(dollars in millions)

Grant Programs and U.S. Code Citation (by Administrative Agency)	FY2008		FY2009		FY2010		FY2011		FY2012	
	Authorized	Enacted	Authorized	Enacted	Authorized	Enacted	Authorized	Enacted	Authorized	Enacted
Office on Violence Against Women (DOJ)										
STOP (Services, Training, Officers, and Prosecutors) Grant Program (42 U.S.C. §3793(a)(18))	$225.00	$183.80	$225.00	$365.00[a]	$225.00	$210.00	$225.00	$209.58	—	$189.00
Grants to Encourage Arrest Policies and Enforcement of Protection Orders (42 U.S.C. §3793(a)(19))	75.00	59.22	75.00	60.00	75.00	60.00	75.00	59.88	—	50.00
Civil Legal Assistance for Victims Grant Program (42 U.S.C. §3796gg-6)	65.00	36.66	65.00	37.00	65.00	41.00	65.00	40.92	—	41.00
Tribal Governments Program (42 U.S.C. §3796gg-10 and 42 U.S.C. §3796gg-1)	[b]	—	[b]	—	[b]	(38.97)	[b]	(37.40)	—	(35.27)
Rural Domestic Violence, Dating Violence, Sexual Assault, Stalking, and Child Abuse Enforcement Assistance (42 U.S.C. §13971)	55.00	40.42	55.00	41.00	55.00	41.00	55.00	40.92	—	34.00
Transitional Housing Assistance Grants for Victims of Domestic Violence (42 U.S.C. §13975)[c]	40.00	(17.39)[d]	40.00	(68.00)[de]	40.00	(18.00)d	40.00	(17.96)[d]	—	25.00
Sexual Assault Services Program (42 U.S.C. §14043g)	50.00	9.40	50.00	12.00	50.00	15.00	50.00	14.97	—	23.00
Grants to State Sexual Assault and Domestic Violence Coalitions Program (42 U.S.C. § 3796gg)	[f]	(10.04)[f]	[f]	(10.58)[f]	[f]	(11.85)f	[f]	(11.83)[f]	—	(11.52)[f]

Grant Programs and U.S. Code Citation (by Administrative Agency)	FY2008		FY2009		FY2010		FY2011		FY2012	
	Authorized	Enacted	Authorized	Enacted	Authorized	Enacted	Authorized	Enacted	Authorized	Enacted
Safe Havens: Supervised Visitation and Support Program (42 U.S.C. §10420)[g]	20.00	13.63	20.00	14.00	20.00	14.00	20.00	13.97	—	11.50
Consolidated Youth Oriented Program[h]	—	—	—	—	—	—	—	—	—	10.00
Grants to Enhance Culturally and Linguistically Specific Services for Victims of Domestic Violence, Dating Violence, Sexual Assault, and Stalking (42 U.S.C. §14045a)	i	(8.30)[i]	i	(8.65)i	i	(9.15)i	i	(9.13)i	—	(9.05)[i]
Grants to Reduce Domestic Violence, Dating Violence, Sexual Assault, and Stalking on Campus Program (42 U.S.C. §14045b)	15.00	9.40	15.00	9.50	15.00	9.50	15.00	9.48	—	9.00
Education, Training and Services to End Violence Against and Abuse of Women with Disabilities (42 U.S.C. §3796gg-7)	10.00	6.58	10.00	6.75	10.00	6.75	10.00	6.74	—	5.75
Court Training and Improvements Program (42 U.S.C. §14043a-3)	5.00	2.80	5.00	3.00	5.00	3.00	5.00	2.99	—	4.50
Enhanced Training and Service to End Violence and Abuse of Women Later in Life Program (42 U.S.C. §14041b)	10.00	4.23	10.00	4.25	10.00	4.25	10.00	4.24	—	4.25
Tribal Domestic Violence and Sexual Assault Coalitions Grant Program (42 U.S.C. §3796gg-1)	j	—	j	—	j	(3.93)k	j	(3.92)[k]	—	(3.93)[k]
Grant for National Resource Center on Workplace Responses to Assist Victims of Domestic and Sexual Violence (42 U.S.C. §14043f)	1.00	0.90	1.00	1.00	1.00	1.00	1.00	1.00	—	1.00

Table A-2. (Continued)

Grant Programs and U.S. Code Citation (by Administrative Agency)	FY2008		FY2009		FY2010		FY2011		FY2012	
	Authorized	Enacted	Authorized	Enacted	Authorized	Enacted	Authorized	Enacted	Authorized	Enacted
Indian Country Sexual Assault Clearinghouse[1]	—	—	—	—	—	—	—	—	—	0.50
Services to Advocate and Respond to Youth (42 U.S.C. §14043c)	15.00	2.82	15.00	3.50	15.00	3.50	15.00	3.49	—	m
Children and Youth Exposed to Violence (42 U.S.C. §14043d-2)	20.00	2.82	20.00	3.00	20.00	3.00	20.00	3.00	—	m
Engaging Men and Youth in Preventing Domestic Violence, Dating Violence, Sexual Assault, and Stalking (42 U.S.C. §14043d-4)	10.00	2.82	10.00	3.00	10.00	3.00	10.00	2.99	—	m
Supporting Teens through Education and Protection (STEP) (42 U.S.C. §14043c-3)	5.00	—	5.00	—	5.00	2.50	5.00	2.50	—	m
Grants to Combat Violence Against Women in Public and Assisted Housing (42 U.S.C. §14043e-4)	10.00	—	10.00	—	10.00	—	10.00	—	—	—
Development of Curricula and Pilot Programs for Home Visitation Projects (42 U.S.C. §14043d-3)	7.00	—	7.00	—	7.00	—	7.00	—	—	—
Access to Justice for Youth (42 U.S.C. §14043c-1)	5.00	—	5.00	—	5.00	—	5.00	—	—	—
Grants to Protect the Privacy and Confidentiality of Victims of Domestic and Dating Violence, Sexual Assault, and Stalking (42 U.S.C. §14043b-4)	5.00	—	5.00	—	5.00	—	5.00	—	—	—

Grant Programs and U.S. Code Citation (by Administrative Agency)	FY2008		FY2009		FY2010		FY2011		FY2012	
	Authorized	Enacted	Authorized	Enacted	Authorized	Enacted	Authorized	Enacted	Authorized	Enacted
Grants for Outreach to Underserved Populations (42 U.S.C. §14045)	2.00	—	2.00	—	2.00	—	2.00	—	—	—
Public Awareness Campaign (42 U.S.C. §14045c)	[n]	—	[n]	—	[n]	—	—	—	—	—
Office of Justice Programs (DOJ)										
Court Appointed Special Advocates for Victims of Child Abuse (42 U.S.C. §13014)	12.00	13.16	12.00	15.00	12.00	15.00	12.00	12.43	—	4.50
Violence Against Women and Family Research and Evaluation Program (NIJ)[o]	[o]	(1.90)	[o]	(1.88)	[o]	(3.00)	[o]	(3.00)	—	3.00
Research on Violence Against Indian Women, National Baseline Study (NIJ) (42 U.S.C. §3796gg– 10 Note)	1.00	0.90	—	1.00	—	1.00	—	0.80	—	1.00
Training Programs to Assist Probation and Parole Officers (42 U.S.C. §13941)	5.00	3.29	5.00	3.50	5.00	3.50	5.00	2.90	—	—
National Stalker and Domestic Violence Reduction (42 U.S.C. §14032)	3.00	2.80	3.00	3.00	3.00	3.00	3.00	2.49	—	—
Tracking of Violence Against Women: National Tribal Sex Offender Registry (28 U.S.C. §534 Note)	1.00	0.90	1.00	1.00	1.00	1.00	1.00	1.00	—	—
Executive Office of U.S. Attorneys (DOJ)										
Federal Victim Assistants[p]	1.00	—	1.00	—	1.00	—	1.00	—	—	—
Undetermined Agency (DOJ)[q]										
Grants for Law Enforcement Training (42 U.S.C. 14044f)	10.00	—	10.00	—	10.00	—	10.00	—	—	—

Table A-2. (Continued)

Grant Programs and U.S. Code Citation (by Administrative Agency)	FY2008		FY2009		FY2010		FY2011		FY2012	
	Authorized	Enacted	Authorized	Enacted	Authorized	Enacted	Authorized	Enacted	Authorized	Enacted
Centers for Disease Control and Prevention (HHS)										
Rape Prevention and Education Grants (42 U.S.C. §280b–1b)	80.00	42.02	80.00	41.84	80.00	42.62	80.00	39.47	—	37.90
Grants to Foster Public Health Responses to Domestic Violence, Dating Violence, Sexual Assault, and Stalking (42 U.S.C. §280g–4)[r]	5.00	—	5.00	—	5.00	—	5.00	—	—	—
Research on Effective Interventions in the Healthcare Setting (42 U.S.C. §13973)[r]	5.00	—	5.00	—	5.00	—	5.00	—	—	—
Study Conducted by the Centers for Disease Control and Prevention (42 U.S.C. §280b–4)	2.00	—	2.00	—	2.00	—	—	—	—	—
Centers for Disease Control and Prevention and Indian Health Service (HHS)										
Analysis and Research on Violence Against Indian Women, Injury Study[s]	0.50	—	0.50	—	—	—	—	—	—	—
Administration for Children and Families (HHS)										
Collaborative Grants to Increase the Long-Term Stability of Victims (42 U.S.C. §14043e–3)	10.00	—	10.00	—	10.00	—	10.00	—	—	—
Grants for Training and Collaboration on the Intersection Between Domestic Violence and Child Maltreatment (Family and Youth Services Bureau) (42 U.S.C. §14043c–2)	5.00	—	5.00	—	5.00	—	5.00	—	—	—

Grant Programs and U.S. Code Citation (by Administrative Agency)	FY2008		FY2009		FY2010		FY2011		FY2012	
	Authorized	Enacted	Authorized	Enacted	Authorized	Enacted	Authorized	Enacted	Authorized	Enacted
Health Resources and Services Administration (HHS)										
Interdisciplinary Training and Education on Domestic Violence and Other Types of Violence and Abuse (42 U.S.C. §294h)[d]	3.00	—	3.00	—	3.00	—	3.00	—	—	—

Source: FY2008–FY2012 appropriations for the OVW and OJP were taken from the congressional budget submissions for the OVW and OJP, and the set-asides for Grants to Enhance Culturally and Linguistically Specific Services for Victims of Domestic Violence, Dating Violence, Sexual Assault, and Stalking and Grants to State Sexual Assault and Domestic Violence Coalitions Program were provided by the OVW. The FY2008 and FY2009 appropriations for the CDC were taken from S.Rept. 110-410. The FY2010-FY2012 appropriations for the CDC were provided by the CDC.

Notes: This table includes programs authorized in the most recent reauthorization of VAWA (P.L. 109-162) and subsequent amendment to VAWA (P.L. 109-271). This table includes VAWA authorized programs that did not receive appropriations. Programs that are funded by set-asides from VAWA authorized programs are reflected in this table and marked with parentheses.

a. This amount includes $225.00 million provided by the American Recovery and Reinvestment Act of 2009 (P.L. 111-5).

b. The Tribal Governments Program is funded by set-asides from seven other OVW grant programs: STOP; Grants to Encourage Arrest Policies and Enforcement of Protection Orders; Rural Domestic Violence, Dating Violence, Sexual Assault, Stalking, and Child Abuse Enforcement Assistance; Civil Legal Assistance for Victims; Safe Havens; Transitional Housing; and Court Training and Improvements.

c. This program was originally authorized by the Prosecutorial Remedies and Other Tools to End the Exploitation of Children Today (PROTECT) Act of 2003 (P.L. 108-21), and was reauthorized by the Violence Against Women and Department of Justice Reauthorization Act of 2005.

d. For FY2008-FY2011, this program was funded by set-asides from the STOP Program.

e. This amount includes emergency supplemental appropriations of $50.00 million provided under The American Recovery and Reinvestment Act of 2009 (P.L. 111-5).

f. The State Coalitions Program is funded by statutory set-asides from the STOP Program and Sexual Assault Services Program.

g. This grant was originally authorized by the Victims of Trafficking and Violence Protection Act of 2000 (P.L. 106-386). It was modified and reauthorized by the Violence Against Women and Department of Justice Reauthorization Act of 2005.

h. This program is not authorized by VAWA. It consolidates four VAWA-authorized programs in the Office on Violence Against Women: Engaging Men and Youth in Prevention, Grants to Assist Children and Youth Exposed to Violence, Supporting Teens Through Education Program (STEP), and Services to Advocate and Respond to Youth.

i. The Culturally and Linguistically Specific Services Program is funded by statutory set-asides from Grants to Encourage Arrest Policies and Enforcement of Protection Orders; Rural Domestic Violence, Dating Violence, Sexual Assault, Stalking Assistance Program; Civil Legal Assistance for Victims; Enhanced Training and Service to End Violence and Abuse of Women Later in Life Program; Sexual Assault Services Program; and Education, Training and Services to End Violence Against and Abuse of Women with Disabilities.

j. Congress did not specify an amount of funding for this program but authorized set-asides from the STOP Program and Sexual Assault Services Program.

k. The Tribal Domestic Violence and Sexual Assault Coalitions Program is funded by statutory set-asides from the STOP Program and Sexual Assault Services Program.

l. This program does not have a U.S. Code citation and is not specifically authorized by VAWA. Congress established this program under the Consolidated and Further Continuing Appropriations Act, 2012 (P.L. 112-55) for the purpose of providing training and technical assistance on issues relating to sexual assault of American Indian and Alaska Native women. It is included in this table because it fulfills a stated purpose of VAWA grant funds directed to Indian country and Alaska native villages.

m. This program is one of four programs consolidated to create the Consolidated Youth Oriented Program. FY2012 funding for this program is reflected in the FY2012 funding for the Consolidated Youth Oriented Program.

n. The Violence Against Women and Department of Justice Reauthorization Act of 2005 authorized "sums as may be necessary" for FY2006-FY2010.

o. This program is not authorized by VAWA. It is included in this table because it was funded by a set-aside from the STOP Program from FY2008-FY2011. In FY2012, it received a direct appropriation.

p. This program does not have a U.S. Code citation but funding is authorized under Sec. 110 of the Violence Against Women and Department of Justice Reauthorization Act of 2005.

q. The Attorney General has not yet determined the administrative office for the Grants for Law Enforcement Training Program.

r. These programs were never funded, however, the basic purpose areas were funded through an appropriations provision with grants administered by the HHS Office of Women's Health (OWH). For additional information, see http://www.womenshealth.gov/violence

s. This program does not have a U.S. Code citation but funding is authorized under Sec. 904 of the Violence Against Women and Department of Justice Reauthorization Act of 2000.

APPENDIX B. SELECTED ISSUES IN VAWA LEGISLATION FROM THE 112TH CONGRESS

In the 112th Congress, bills (S. 1925 and H.R. 4970) were passed in each chamber that would have reauthorized most of the programs under VAWA, among other things. H.R. 4970 differed in substantive ways from S. 1925.

As the VAWA bills were being debated, several issues surfaced, including

- whether the cap on the number of U visas available for nonimmigrants should be increased temporarily;
- whether the certification process for U visa applicants should be amended to include additional requirements;
- whether new restrictions should be placed on nonimmigrant victims seeking to obtain legal status;
- whether the Lesbian, Gay, Bisexual, and Transgender (LGBT) population should be included in the definition as an underserved population;
- whether American Indian tribes should be given increased jurisdictional power over domestic violence cases involving non-tribal victims and/or perpetrators; and
- the accountability of VAWA grant recipients.

S. 1925 proposed to temporarily increase the cap on the number of U visas available for battered nonimmigrants (from 10,000 to 15,000).[70] U visas grant nonimmigrant status to nonimmigrants who are victims of domestic violence and are willing to assist authorities in the investigation and prosecution of their attackers.[71] H.R. 4970, however, would have kept the U visa capped at 10,000 and would have made the visa temporary.[72] Proponents contended that the temporary increase proposed in S. 1925 is necessary because of the delays involved in the issuance of these visas.[73] Opponents contended that providing a specific pathway to citizenship for this population is not fair to the large number of foreign nationals who are waiting in line for their turn.[74]

The House bill contained provisions that were aimed at preventing fraud in the VAWA self- petition and U visa process. For example, with respect to VAWA benefits, the bill would have required nonimmigrant victims to submit to an in-person interview and adjudicating officers to consider all credible evidence, among other things. With respect to obtaining legal permanent residence status through the U visa, the House bill would have required, as part of the law enforcement certification process, the commencement of the related criminal investigation and prosecution. Also, the bill would have required the nonimmigrant victim to provide information on the identity of the alleged abuser.[75] Immigrant advocates contended that the proposed requirements would have deterred nonimmigrant victims from reporting these crimes.

The Senate bill contained a provision that would add persons who may be discriminated against based on sexual orientation or gender identity as an "underserved population" under VAWA. Critics contended that data are needed to support providing protected status to the LGBT population. Some also held that current law doesn't exclude the LGBT population from receiving federally funded resources.[76]

S. 1925 proposed to increase jurisdictional power for American Indian tribes by granting tribes the civil authority to issue and enforce protection orders over any person. Also, the bill would have created a pilot program permitting tribes to have criminal jurisdiction over cases involving domestic violence. Critics contended that such actions would have represented an unprecedented expansion of tribal jurisdiction, and defendants may not receive the full panoply of constitutional protections.[77]

Another issue raised in opposition to S. 1925 was the lack of accountability for VAWA grantees.[78] Over the last few years, the DOJ Office of the Inspector General has audited several OVW grantees. The audit reports have cited improper allocation of funds, untimely financial and progress reports, weaknesses in budget management, and other compliance issues.[79] Additionally, the GAO has released several reports more broadly assessing DOJ grant management and oversight. While S. 1925 would have required the OVW to establish a biennial conferral process with grantees and key stakeholders, a concern was raised that the proposed legislation would not have adequately ensured accountability of grant recipients.[80] H.R. 4970 sought to address issues of accountability by including provisions that would have required the Inspector Generals of DOJ and HHS to conduct annual audits of at least 10% of all VAWA grant recipients.

Also, the House bill would have required grantees to submit information regarding other federal grants they have applied for during the preceding year and provide a list of federal grants they received during the five-year period preceding the current application.

End Notes

[1] Kathleen Maguire and Ann Pastore, *Sourcebook of Criminal Justice Statistics 1994*, Bureau of Justice Statistics, Tables 3.108, 3.131, http://www.albany.edu/sourcebook/pdf/sb1994/sb1994-section3.pdf; and U.S. Department of Justice, Federal Bureau of Investigation, *Crime in the United States*, http://www.fbi.gov/about-us/cjis/ucr/ucr. Violent crimes include murders, non-negligent manslaughters, and aggravated assaults.

[2] Kimberley D. Bailey, "Lost in Translation: Domestic Violence, "the Personal is Political," and the Criminal Justice System.," *Journal of Criminal Law & Criminology*, vol. 100, no. 4 (Fall 2010), pp. 1255-1300.

[3] Murray Straus and Richard Gelles, "Societal Change and Change in Family Violence from 1975 to 1985," *Journal of Marriage and Family*, vol. 48, Iss. 3, August 1986.

[4] Ibid.

[5] Senators Biden and Boxer, "Violence Against Women," Remarks in the Senate, *Congressional Record*, June 21, 1994.

[6] Joseph Biden, "Violence Against Women: The Congressional Response," *American Psychologist*, vol. 48, no. 10 (October 1993), pp. 1059-1061; Barbara Vobejda, "Battered Women's Cry Relayed Up From Grass Roots," *The Washington Post*, July 6, 1994, p. A1.

[7] Fed. R. Evid. 412.

[8] In 2000, the U.S. Supreme Court struck down a provision of VAWA that allowed for a civil remedy for victims of gender-based violence. For more information, see *U.S. v. Morrison*, 529 U.S. 598 (2000).

[9] 42 U.S.C. §10401 et seq.

[10] 42 U.S.C. §280b et seq.

[11] 42 U.S.C. §5711 et seq.

[12] The National Domestic Violence Hotline is now authorized by FVPSA (P.L. 111-320) and codified at 42 U.S.C. §10413.

[13] For more information, see CRS Report R42477, *Immigration Provisions of the Violence Against Women Act (VAWA)*, by William A. Kandel.

[14] In 2002, OVW was codified through Title IV of the 21st Century Department of Justice Appropriations Authorization Act (P.L. 107-273).

[15] U.S. Department of Justice, Office on Violence Against Women, *About the Office*, http://www.ovw.usdoj.gov/ overview.htm.

[16] Shannan Catalano, Erica Smith, Howard Snyder, and Michael Rand, U.S. Department of Justice, Bureau of Justice Statistics, *Female Victims of Violence*, September 2009, http://bjs.ojp.usdoj.gov/content/pub/pdf/fvv.pdf (hereinafter *Female Victims of Violence*, 2009); and Katrina Baum, Shannan Catalano, and Michael Rand, U.S. Department of Justice, Bureau of Justice Statistics, *Stalking Victimization in the United States - Revised*, September 2012, http://www.bjs.gov/content/pub/pdf/svus_rev.pdf (hereinafter *Stalking Victimization in the United States - Revised*, 2012).

[17] The Centers for Disease Control and Prevention, *Youth Risk Behavior Surveillance System: Selected 2011 National Health Risk Behaviors and Health Outcomes by Sex*, http://www.cdc.gov/healthyyouth/yrbs/pdf/ us_disparitysex_yrbs.pdf.

[18] U.S. Department of Health and Human Services, The Centers for Disease Control, *Youth Risk Behavior Surveillance System (YRBSS)*, http://www.cdc.gov/healthyyouth/yrbs/; and U.S. Department of Justice, Office of Justice Programs, Bureau of Justice Statistics, *National Crime Victimization Survey*, http://bjs.ojp.usdoj.gov/index.cfm?ty=dcdetail&iid= 245.

[19] U.S. Department of Justice, Federal Bureau of Investigation, *Uniform Crime Reporting Program*, http://www.fbi.gov/about-us/cjis/ucr/ucr.

[20] For additional information regarding the differences in crime data collection and limitations of the data, see CRS Report RL34309, *How Crime in the United States Is Measured*, by Nathan James and Logan Rishard Council. For a comparison of methodologies used by the

UCR and National Crime Victimization Survey, see *The Nation's Two Crime Measures*, http://bjs.ojp.usdoj.gov/content/pub/pdf/ntcm.pdf.

[21] U.S. Congress, House Committee on the Judiciary, Subcommittee on Crime, Terrorism, and Homeland Security, *Hearing on: the U.S. Department of Justice, Office on Violence Against Women*, Testimony by Susan Carbon, 112th Cong., 2nd sess., February 16, 2012.

[22] 42 U.S.C. §13925.

[23] Shannan Catalano, U.S. Department of Justice, Bureau of Justice Statistics, *Intimate Partner Violence, 1993 – 2010*, http://www.bjs.gov/index.cfm?ty=pbdetail&iid=4536.

[24] Ibid, p. 2.

[25] The CDC provided the following examples of severe physical violence: "hit with a fist or something hard, beaten, [or] slammed against something."

[26] The Centers for Disease Control and Prevention, *National Intimate Partner Sexual Violence Survey, 2010 Summary Report*, November 2011, p. 2, http://www.cdc.gov/ViolencePrevention/pdf/NISVS_Executive_Summary-a.pdf (hereinafter *National Intimate Partner Sexual Violence Survey, 2010*).

[27] Laura Dugan, Daniel Nagin, and Richard Rosenfeld, Do Domestic Violence Services Save Lives?, *National Institute of Justice Journal*, Issue 250 (November 2003), p. 22, https://www.ncjrs.gov/pdffiles1/jr000250f.pdf.

[28] Ibid.

[29] Margaret Zahn, Intimate Partner Homicide: An Overview, *National Institute of Justice Journal*, Issue 250 (November 2003), p. 2; and Bureau of Justice Statistics, *Homicide Trends in the United States, 1980-2008*, November 2011, pp. 3, 18, http://bjs.ojp.usdoj.gov/content/pub/pdf/htus8008.pdf (hereinafter *Homicide Trends in the United States*).

[30] *Homicide Trends in the United States*, p. 10.

[31] *Female Victims of Violence*, 2009. p. 2.

[32] 42 U.S.C. §13925; 18 U.S.C. §2241 et seq.

[33] U.S. Department of Justice, Bureau of Justice Statistics, *Criminal Victimization, 2010*, September 2011, p. 9, http://bjs.ojp.usdoj.gov/content/pub/pdf/cv10.pdf.

[34] U.S. Department of Justice, Federal Bureau of Investigation, *Crime in the United States, 2010*, September 2011, p.1, http://www.fbi.gov/about-us/cjis/ucr/crime-in-the-u.s/2010/crime-in-the-u.s.-2010/violent-crime/rapemain.pdf.

[35] Ibid.

[36] U.S. Department of Justice, Office of Public Affairs, *Attorney General Eric Holder Announces Revisions to the Uniform Crime Report's Definition of Rape*, http://www.justice.gov/opa/pr/2012/January/12-ag-018.html.

[37] 42 U.S.C. §13925.

[38] Ibid.

[39] The Centers for Disease Control and Prevention, *Trends in the Prevalence of Behaviors that Contribute to Violence National YRBS: 1991–2011*, http://www.cdc.gov/healthyyouth/yrbs/pdf/us_violence

[40] The Centers for Disease Control and Prevention, *Youth Risk Behavior Surveillance System: Selected 2011 National Health Risk Behaviors and Health Outcomes by Sex*, http://www.cdc.gov/healthyyouth/yrbs/pdf/ us_disparitysex_yrbs.pdf.

[41] *Stalking Victimization in the United States - Revised*, 2012, p. 1.

[42] Ibid.

[43] 18 U.S.C. §2261(A).

[44] In 2006, the NCVS included a supplemental survey that identified victims of stalking.

[45] *Stalking Victimization in the United States - Revised*, 2012, pp. 3-4.

[46] *National Intimate Partner Sexual Violence Survey, 2010*, p. 2.

[47] In 2000, the House passed the Victims of Trafficking and Violence Protection Act of 2000 (P.L. 106-386) with a 371-1 vote and the Senate unanimously passed the bill. In 2005, the House passed the Violence Against Women and Department of Justice Reauthorization Act of 2005 (P.L. 109-162) with a 415-4 vote, and the Senate again unanimously passed the bill.

[48] For more information, see CRS Report R42477, *Immigration Provisions of the Violence Against Women Act (VAWA)*, by William A. Kandel.

[49] The term "dating violence" was not used in the original VAWA and was added in VAWA 2000.

[50] 18 U.S.C. §2261 and §2262.

[51] Provisions in VAWA 2005 were modified in A Bill to Make Technical Corrections to the Violence Against Women and Department of Justice Reauthorization Act of 2005 (P.L. 109-271).

[52] For more information, see CRS Report R42477, *Immigration Provisions of the Violence Against Women Act (VAWA)*, by William A. Kandel.

[53] While the expiration of VAWA has no legal effect on the authority of the federal government to carry out VAWA programs and activities, it may have procedural ramifications for congressional consideration of appropriations acts that provide funding for the projects and activities authorized by VAWA. For general information on procedural and legal issues related to the authorization of appropriations, see CRS Report R42098, *Authorization of Appropriations: Procedural and Legal Issues*, by Jessica Tollestrup and Brian T. Yeh.

[54] Prior to passage of S. 47, the Senate passed S.Amdt. 10, S.Amdt. 11, and S.Amdt. 21.

[55] The authorization levels for existing VAWA grant programs would either decrease or remain the same.

[56] S. 47 would allow sharing of law enforcement-generated and prosecution-generated information necessary for law enforcement or prosecution.

[57] S. 47 would define a population specific organization as a "nonprofit, nongovernmental organization that primarily serves members of a specific underserved population and has demonstrated experience and expertise providing targeted services to members of that specific underserved population."
S. 47 would define population specific services as "victim-centered services that address the safety, health, economic, legal, housing, workplace, immigration, confidentiality, or other needs of victims of domestic violence, dating violence, sexual assault, or stalking, and that are designed primarily for and are targeted to a specific underserved population."

[58] 42 U.S.C. §14135.

[59] The Debbie Smith DNA Backlog Grant Program provides grants to state and local governments for five major purposes: (1) conducting analyses of DNA samples collected under applicable legal authority for inclusion in the NDIS, (2) conducting analyses of forensic DNA samples for inclusion in the NDIS, (3) increasing the capacity of state and local laboratories to carry out DNA analyses, (4) collecting DNA samples from people required to submit them and forensic samples from crimes, and (5) ensuring that analyses of forensic DNA samples are carried out in a timely manner. For more information on Debbie Smith grants, see CRS Report R41800, *DNA Testing in Criminal Justice: Background, Current Law, Grants, and Issues*, by Nathan James.

[60] The Combined DNA Index System (CODIS) searches three indexes (convicted offenders, arrestee, and forensic) to generate investigative leads. The convicted offender index contains DNA profiles developed from samples collected from convicted offenders; the arrestee index contains DNA profiles developed from samples collected from arrested but not yet convicted individuals; and the forensic index contains DNA profiles developed from samples collected at crime scenes. CODIS searches across these indexes to look for potential matches. For more information, see U.S. Department of Justice, DNA Initiative: DNA Databases, http://www.dna.gov/dna-databases/levels.

[61] 42 U.S.C. §113.

[62] 42 U.S.C. §13925 defines underserved populations as "populations underserved because of geographic location, underserved racial and ethnic populations, populations underserved because of special needs (such as language barriers, disabilities, alienage status, or age), and any other population determined to be underserved by the Attorney General or by the Secretary of Health and Human Services, as appropriate."

[63] The areas of conferral would include (1) the administration of grants, (2) unmet needs, (3) promising practices in the field, and (4) emerging trends. After the conferral with grantees, OVW would be required to publish a comprehensive report that summarizes the issues presented and what, if any, policies it intends to implement to address those issues.

[64] As submitted by abused foreign nationals who are seeking lawful permanent resident status.

[65] For additional information, see CRS Report R42477, *Immigration Provisions of the Violence Against Women Act (VAWA)*, by William A. Kandel.

[66] Tribes do not currently have criminal jurisdiction over non-Indians (*Oliphant v. Suquamish Indian Tribe*, 435 U.S. (191, 210 1978). Both bills would expand tribal courts' criminal jurisdiction over non-Indians for crimes of domestic violence. For additional information, see CRS Report R42488, *Tribal Criminal Jurisdiction over Non-Indians in S. 47 and H.R. 11, the Violence Against Women Reauthorization Act of 2013*, by Jane M. Smith and Richard M. Thompson II.

[67] In S. 47, the provision would not apply to Indian tribes in the state of Alaska, with the exception of two Indian tribes.

[68] In S. 47, several VAWA grant programs (42 U.S.C. 14043c through 14043c–3) would be consolidated into one youth oriented program known as the Creating Hope through Outreach, Options, Services, and Education for Children and Youth.

[69] For more information regarding the Trafficking Victims Protection Act of 2000 and trafficking in persons, see CRS Report RL34317, *Trafficking in Persons: U.S. Policy and Issues for Congress*, by Alison Siskin and Liana Sun Wyler.

[70] The legislation proposed to recapture unused visas that were available and not issued to nonimmigrants from 2006 – 2011. For additional information regarding U visas and VAWA provisions related to immigrant status, see CRS Report R42477, *Immigration Provisions of the Violence Against Women Act (VAWA)*, by William A. Kandel.

[71] 8 U.S.C. §1101(a)(15).

[72] S.Rept. 112-153. Under current law, the U visa allows certain nonimmigrant victims of crime a pathway to permanent residence status.

[73] This particular provision was included in the VAWA 2005 reauthorization bill, however, regulations were not implemented until 2008, which created a large number of unused U Visas between 2006 and 2008. There were additional unused U Visas between 2009 and 2011. See Table C-1 in CRS Report R42477, *Immigration Provisions of the Violence Against Women Act (VAWA)*, by William A. Kandel.

[74] See S.Rept. 112-153.

[75] For information on the certification process and a more in depth discussion of the issues as they pertain to VAWA reauthorization, see CRS Report R42477, *Immigration Provisions of the Violence Against Women Act (VAWA)*, by William A. Kandel.

[76] U.S. Congress, House Committee on the Judiciary, *Violence Against Women A Reauthorization Act of 2012*, H.Rept. 112-480, 112th Cong., 2nd sess., May 15, 2012.

[77] Although tribes are not bound by protections found in the U.S. Constitution (*Talton v. Mayes*, 163 U.S. 376 (1896)), there are similar statutory protections for criminal defendants in tribal courts. See 25 U.S.C. §1302(6). For additional information, see CRS Report R42488, *Tribal Criminal Jurisdiction over Non-Indians in S. 47 and H.R. 11, the Violence Against Women Reauthorization Act of 2013*, by Jane M. Smith and Richard M. Thompson II.

[78] S.Rept. 112-153.

[79] U.S. Department of Justice, Office of the Inspector General, Audit of the Office on Violence Against Women Cooperative Agreement Administered by Girls Educational and Mentoring Services: New York, New York, GR-70-12- 003, March 2012, http://www.justice.gov/oig/grantsAudit of the Office on Violence Against Women Grants to Jane Doe, Inc.: Boston, Massachusetts, GR-70-11-005, August 2011, http://www.justice.gov/oig/grants/2011/g7011005r.pdf; Audit of Office on Violence Against Women Grants Awarded to the Montana Coalition Against Domestic and Sexual Violence: Helena, Montana, GR-60-11-001, October 2010, http://www.justice.gov/oig/ grants/2010/g6011001.pdf; Office on

Violence Against Women Services, Training, Officers, and Prosecution Grants Awarded to the Commonwealth of Virginia Department of Criminal Justice Services, GR-30-10-003, July 2010, http://www.justice.gov/oig/grants/2010/g3010003.pdf; and Office on Violence Against Women Legal Assistance for Victims Grant Program Administered by the Community Legal Aid Society, Inc.: Wilmington, DE, GR-70-10-005, July 2010.

[80] S.Rept. 112-153.

INDEX